A Parent's Guide to
Coaching
Baseball

A Parent's Guide to
Coaching Baseball

John P. McCarthy, Jr.

BETTERWAY PUBLICATIONS, INC.
WHITE HALL, VIRGINIA

Published by Betterway Publications, Inc.
P.O. Box 219
Crozet, VA 22932
(804) 823-5661

Cover design and photographs by Susan Riley
Typography by Park Lane Associates

Library of Congress Cataloging-in-Publication Data

McCarthy, John P.
    A parent's guide to coaching baseball / John P. McCarthy, Jr.
        p.   cm.
    Includes index.
    ISBN: 1-55870-124-9 $7.95
    1. Baseball for children--Coaching.   I. Title
GV880.4.M37   1989
796.357'62--dc20
                                                            89-36140
                                                            CIP

Printed in the United States of America
0 9 8 7 6 5 4

To Linda, Jackie, Michelle, and Joey, and to kids everywhere.
Why I coach, why I am.

CONTENTS

PREFACE.. 9

1. HITTING.. 13

Ya Gotta Believe!, 13
Hitting, Hitting, Hitting, 15
The Basics — How to Hit, 17
Summary and Other Tips, 33
Switch Hitting, 36
Bunting, 37

2. FIELDING.. 39

Catching, 40
Throwing, 47
The Cut-off and Throwing
   Ahead of the Lead Runner, 51
Rundowns, 55

3. RULES OF THE GAME............................. 57

Field Dimensions and General Rules, 57
Glossary: Let's Talk Baseball, 61

4. RUNNING AND SLIDING........................... 67

Running Bases, 68
Stealing Bases, 70
Sliding, 70

5. BASEBALL POSITIONS............................ **75**

Catcher, 75
First Base, 80
Second Base, 83
Shortstop, 87
Third Base, 90
Outfield, 91
Pitcher, 94

6. ODDS AND ENDS................................... **105**

The Best Age to Learn the Game, 105
Winning, Winning, Winning, 106
How Can I Get My Kid Interested in Baseball?, 107
Behavior at Games, 107
How to Deal with the Coach, 108
Warming Up, 109

7. PARENT'S CHECKLIST **111**

Hitting, 111
Fielding, 113
Running and Sliding, 114
Baseball Positions, 114

POEM: Oh My Gosh, I'm Up!.......................... **119**

INDEX.. **123**

PREFACE

"What's he doing wrong?" The expression on Dave's face was dead serious, very concerned. I could hear the frustration in his voice. His son was ten years old. As a nine year old the season before he had not gotten a hit, not one. Now, a few weeks into the new season, he was still not hitting. Dave pleaded, "It's really beginning to bother him. What can I do?"

I can't tell you how many times I've been asked these questions. And why not? Baseball is our biggest and most popular sport, as American as a hot dog. Most parents want their kids to have fun with it, to do well. And some just don't want to be embarrassed in front of the other parents.

The trouble with baseball's popularity is that a lot of coaches are needed, but very few are trained or knowledgeable. When I started fifteen years ago, I knew nothing about coaching. Sure, I played baseball as a kid, and softball later on, but I knew nothing about coaching. Very few parents do when they volunteer to coach a team. Fortunately they do volunteer, but often they either don't know the basics or don't know how to coach them.

So I went to the bookstore for some help. However, most books were about big league baseball, written by big league experts. Coaching eight, nine, ten year old kids is completely different. Their needs are different. Big league coaches only deal with yesterday's Little League all-stars. They have no idea how to get a below average ten year old to hang in there. I remember wishing that there was a good book for parents. One that better understood the special needs of children and that a parent could easily understand.

After all, parents are the ones who most influence whether a boy or girl will improve and stay with the game. That's right, we parents! We decide not to drive them to practice and, if the field is too far away, they don't play . . . maybe never play. Or, when sign-up time comes and they are a bit hesitant, our lack of support will end the question. On the other hand, if we decide to get up and throw a few pitches to our kids at an early age, it just may be that one day we have a ball player in the family. Most important, it is the parent who can help a kid to believe that he or she is a hitter and that hitting baseballs is easy and fun. By knowing a few basics, you can help mold a good bat swing, or at least prevent bad habits from developing. I've seen some of these bad habits, and I've seen them take years to fix.

In today's Little League circles, parents have gotten a bad reputation. I recently chatted with a lifelong friend of my father's about this book. "Uncle Load" was always a good athlete, and spent his later years coaching and administering youth sports. He laughed and told me, "Jackie, when it comes to parents there are two rules. The first rule is 'No Parents', and the second rule is remember the first rule." In fact, when the subject comes up in conversation, people say, "Yeah, too bad about the way parents act, ruins everything."

Then it occurred to me that in all my years of coaching, I rarely had a parent problem. I figured it must be because I involved parents from the start. I got them directly involved with helping the coaching. I'd tell them what to do and what to look for. They became knowledgeable, part of the team, and best of all, they learned how to coach their children on their own.

I'm not saying that just being supportive is not enough. It is more than many kids get from their folks. But you can go further if you want to, much further. This book gives you that option. It will give you enough to be a pretty decent coach if you want to be one, or it will give you enough background just to help your child improve and hang in there. Whatever you do, it's going to make a difference. You will feel like a better parent, and your son or daughter will become a better ballplayer. Best of all, you and your child will become friends, just from playing together.

I coached my older son in Little League for six years. Then, after a six year stint as coach of my daughter's soccer team, I returned to baseball to coach my youngest son. I've also coached basketball. Over the years I've learned a great deal about kids and parents. I've also learned lots of hints, tips, and gimmicks on how to get kids going, get them to improve. They are all here in this book. They work! All of the teams I have coached have been winning teams, including several championship teams. My teams were always known for their hitting. Not that I emphasize winning, I don't. I emphasize confidence, improvement, and team spirit. These things lead to winning. I'm convinced that there is a way to get every single kid going if he wants to, to get him feeling good about his ability. That's why I coach, that's why I wrote this book.

To Kids
Jack McCarthy

1.

HITTING

Hitting is the most important part of baseball, and it's definitely the most fun. An old ballplayer once told me, "Defense is something you have to do while you are waiting to get up at bat again." Sure, fielding, running, and throwing are big parts of the game, no doubt about it. But hitting is "numero uno," so that's where we start!

Many coaches, especially big league coaches, will tell you that you either have it as a hitter or you don't. They will quote statistics showing that a player's average is generally highest early in his pro career, suggesting that there is usually little or no improvement from year to year. Well, that may be true for the big leagues, maybe even college, and perhaps high school (though I doubt it). But it is absolutely dead wrong for children. Kids can improve tremendously. I've seen it countless times. I've also seen kids get much worse. This tells me one thing loud and clear — coaching helps, and parents count, parents can make the difference.

YA GOTTA BELIEVE!

This is the most important concept in this whole book. If hitting is the life of baseball, then confidence is its soul. If you can help your child to the point where he believes he is a good hitter, so that he expects to hit the ball when he gets up, then you have planted a seed whose growth cannot be denied. We want him to get up thinking about where the ball will go, not whether he will hit it.

You have to tell them that they are already hitters. That there is a hitter inside them, maybe waiting to come out, maybe needing some help, some instruction, some experience, but definitely a hitter. At my first practice every year, that's just what I do. I tell my players they are hitters, I have them say it, I keep saying it. I make a fuss when someone makes good contact with the ball. The sound or "crack" of a well hit ball is distinctive. I point it out to the kids, and pretty soon everybody is listening for it.

It's not a lie, not even a fib, not at the Little League level. All kids are hitters. Hitting is easy, it's natural. The problems come when fear or doubt get involved and interfere with the hitter. Never, never, never, criticize your child in a way that tells her she is not a hitter. If you do, she may never become the hitter she already is. Just say to your child, "You are a hitter, I know you are. We're almost there. It's coming, ya gotta believe!" Then when it does come (and it will), she swings the bat nicely or makes good contact (the first sign of improvement) — you let the whole world know about it. Make a kid feel proud and confident of herself, and her ability will blossom like a whole field of flowers.

Last season I had a boy named Matt on the team, a ten year old. I coached him as an eight year old, and drafted him back this year because I liked him. This boy was motivated. He wanted to be a good hitter in the worst way. He had a tough season the year before, and he was having similar troubles early in this season, swinging too hard, trying too hard. He would strike out and start crying.

I told him it was okay to cry, no problem. It just showed how much he wanted to hit, and that was fine. I kept telling him that he was a hitter, that it would come, it was just around the corner. "Just relax a bit, Matt, control your energy. It'll come." And it did by mid-season. The hits came and with them a smile you could float on and a gleam in his mother's eye like sunshine. He really expected to hit the ball, and when that happens the hits are coming, no way will they be denied.

The worst problem with kids who are not hitting is often not their style of swinging; that's usually easy to fix. The main problems are fear and doubt. The two feed off each other. A kid will start off afraid that he is going to get hit by the pitcher. This occurs at about eight or nine when kids start pitching. The fear causes a defensive swing, or stepping back until they can't even reach the ball. Then, after a lot of hitless at bats, self-doubt takes over. They think they can't do it. They become afraid of being embarrassed in front of friends and parents. Now they have three problems: fear, self-doubt, and a lousy swing. You have to face these problems head on. Tell them they can do it, that it's easy, that they are a hitter, and that improvement is going to come as sure as the morning sun. Ya gotta believe!

Start with just a spark of confidence, then mold a good swing from that. It's natural to hit as long as the kid isn't fighting himself. Get rid of the negatives, focus on the positive, and things will happen the way they are supposed to happen. Good hitters think it's easy to hit; ask them, they are the ones who know!

HITTING, HITTING, HITTING

Practice, Practice, Practice

Well, if confidence is the soul of baseball, then repetition is its backbone. I've had a lot of winning teams in baseball and the main reason is lots of hitting practice. Emphasize hitting! I remember talking to one parent, and after his nine year old was swinging the bat nicely, I said to him, "He has a nice swing, now he just needs to hit a few hundred balls." Too often parents just go out and play catch with the child. No problem, but remember that hitting is "numero uno" and should be included, even emphasized.

The more your boy or girl practices HITTING, the better he or she is going to be, especially at Little League age. Somebody has to pitch to them, practice with them. This is where you come in. Get a couple of balls and throw to them. Using several balls will save time chasing after them, unless you have an eager second child for that task. I have a whole bucket of balls that I use.

Don't worry about how well you can pitch — you will improve too! Throw the ball close at first, from twenty-five to thirty-five feet away if that initially helps your control. Move back to forty-six feet when you can. Up to nine years old thirty-five feet or less is fine, from nine onward you want to get to forty-six feet as soon as possible. And make it fun! When I do it with my son Joey, I have a marker on the field (lawn, street, lot, whatever) for the farthest distance he hits a ball that day. Have your child try to hit to different fields, right, center, and left. Twenty to thirty pitches is okay, more is better. Mickey Mantle's father used to pitch to him all the time, his brother chased down the balls. Repetition works, guaranteed!

Another idea is to take your child to an area batting cage. I use them all the time, I even got my own father out the other day to hit a few at the cage at Seaside Heights, NJ. We all had fun, and it didn't cost much. He hit the pants off the ball, sixty-two years old! There should be a cage within a half-hour drive (I've driven up to an hour with my team each way). In some areas indoor cages are springing up, and they are great for rainy days. They usually have a slow and medium speed cage for children. First watch for a minute and pick out the best speed for your child. Eleven and twelve year olds should hit a 45 m.p.h. pitch. Start slow and build up speed. It's about a dollar for twenty balls, sometimes $1.25. Three dollars worth, sixty balls, is a thorough workout, and is about the most you should do. Also, bring your own bat if you have one, the grips are usually lousy on batting cage bats. A batter's glove is also very useful as the hand can get sore from a good workout. They have helmets — ask for one. Take a break after each twenty balls and talk about her swing, or watch other batters. The idea is to do a lot of hitting — it's the key to it all. Have her take swings lefty (if she is righty) and bunt a few, too. Take some swings yourself! Give a holler when she makes good contact.

THE BASICS — HOW TO HIT

A dozen years ago, an eight year old got up to the plate. You could see that he was uncomfortable, didn't really know what to do. He chopped at the first pitch for a strike, and his coach started yelling, "C'mon, hit the ball, hit the ball." The next pitch came in, and the boy missed it by over a foot. Again the coach started screaming, "Hit the ball, c'mon, hit the ball." Finally, the kid turned in frustration and shrieked to his coach, "All right, but how? I'm trying, but how?"

I walked up to the boy. At that age the coaches all helped each other, and I knew his parents. "No problem Scott, just keep your eye on it. Watch it leave the pitcher's hand, and watch it until it's in front of you, right over the plate. Don't take your eyes off it." On the next pitch, he hit the ball. He popped out, but he hit the ball. After he turned to go to the dugout, he flashed a big grin at me — it made my day! Saying general things like "hit the ball" is not helpful. Yell out some of the basics like "see the whole ball," "keep your head down," "keep your hands up," "hard bat," or "don't drop your right shoulder." These things are helpful. The next sections will discuss such specifics in detail.

It's a big help to be supportive, to raise confidence, and to practice with your child. If that's all you do, it's still a great help. But the knowledge of some hitting basics, working with your child on her swing, will reap immediate and permanent rewards for both of you.

Keep Your Eye on the Ball

IMPORTANT! Most kids don't usually "see" the pitch until it's about one-third of the way to them. Then they start their swing, and don't see the ball for the last six feet. This means that they only see the ball for roughly half of the time it's in flight, less than a split second. No way your child is going to hit the ball if he doesn't see it, not hit it hard anyway. The most important thing you can say when you practice with your child, or at a game when he is up is simply, "Keep your eye on the ball! Watch it leave the pitcher's hand, all the way to the bat!"

There are a couple of hints you can try. I remember when my eldest son, Jackie, was nine years old. There was a boy named Ray on our team. He was a big kid, very quiet, and not particularly sure of himself. But he had a big heart, and wanted to play ball.

During the season, he hadn't gotten many hits. He was tight when he swung, and he didn't swing often. During one game he had struck out a few times, and then he was up late in the game. The score was close so I had to get him to swing. I called "time out" from my third base coaching spot, and went over to talk to him. I said "Ray, you're a hitter, so I want you to do something for me, I want you to swing at every pitch. This guy is good and he'll get the ball over the plate. Also, I want you to see which way the ball is spinning as it comes towards you, and tell me after each pitch." Well, he took the first pitch over the centerfielder's head, and as he ran to first base (he watched the ball first for a full three seconds, everybody was screaming at him to run) he turned to me, raised his hand, and pointed his finger, rotating it in a clockwise direction. He was telling me which way the ball was spinning! We had found a way to get him to look closely at the ball, and he got a big hit. Of course, he was so long getting around the bases, that he got tagged out at home (I had to send him!), but I don't think he ever knew it — everybody was cheering so loudly. His family moved after the season, and we got Christmas cards for a few years. My wife went back to college last year, and guess who she had in one class — Ray, big as a house!

So look at your son's eyes and head when he swings — if he lifts his head or turns it with his shoulders as he swings, he is not looking at the ball long enough. Tell him to try to see the ball while it's still in the pitcher's hand, so he can be sure to watch it from the start. He must also see the ball in front of him, until the bat hits it. Tell him to keep his head still and try to see the bat hit the ball. He should be looking right down his arms, along the bat. He won't be able to actually see the bat hit it, but he'll watch the ball long enough to hit it.

So those are the three hints: watch it leave the pitcher's hand, watch it closely enough to see it spin as it comes towards the plate, and try to see it hit the bat. Then tell him to run, because he will hit it!

The Stance

The stance is the batting position your child assumes when waiting for the pitch. First of all, if you watch a pro baseball game you will see eighteen different stances. Don Baylor likes to get close to the plate to pull the ball to left field. That's why he gets hit by pitches so often. Pete Rose bent way forward so his head was right in the strike zone, he "saw" the ball very well, and that's why he is the all-time leader in hits. A lot of guys, including Rod Carew, point their bat right at the ump, and they swing very level, slapping out a lot of singles — high batting average but no real power. Some spread their legs wide, some close, some have the right foot planted back a bit, some the left. In 1986 Don Mattingly used to "pigeon toe" his back foot a bit, to get more power. For some reason he stopped in 1988, and he had a bad year slugging. Jack Clark does the opposite, he points his back foot at the ump, and he also holds the bat high over his head as the ball is being pitched. Mel Ott used to lift up his left foot so high when he swung that he looked like he was about to fall down.

So the key to a stance is to let the kid be comfortable — this is one area where you give your child some freedom to do it his way. I'm not saying that there isn't a "right" stance, and I'm going to tell you what it is. There are clearly some important "don'ts" I'll touch on. I'm just saying that hitting is less affected by the stance than by other things, so here is an area where you can allow room for some personal style. Kids are built differently, so different styles may be comfortable.

At very young ages, your child will try to face you as you pitch the ball. It looks cute, but you must gently insist that he stand sideways. Second, they tend to hold the bat right in front of the breastbone. So you need to have him move the bat further back, near his right (for righties) shoulder, hands up even with the shoulder. Tell him to "look like a hitter." Then, when he begins to lapse back into an improper stance, just repeat the phrase "look like a hitter" and watch as he snaps into a correct stance. The main thing in a stance is to keep the hands up and back. At the very least make sure your child does this.

Some coaches put way too much emphasis on stance. They

can really screw up a kid, so much that the kid seems to forget how to swing at all. I've seen coaches do nothing but work on a kid's stance, and by the time they are done the kid swings the bat like she is wrestling a shadow. It's okay to aim for the "correct" stance, just don't try too much at once. Work with one thing at a time, from the context of her present stance.

What is a "correct" stance? The following is for righties, do the opposite for lefties. (See Figures 1 and 2.)

1. Keep the feet a bit wider than shoulder distance apart. If the feet are close together you get more power, since you take a bigger stride towards the ball. However, this also means the body is lunging, so you lose some bat control. If the feet are spread wide, you get the opposite — less lunge, less power, but more control. Tell her to adjust to what's comfortable, what works best. A key is to feel balanced.

2. The left foot should never be past the plate, towards the pitcher. Usually, the farther she stands back in the batter's box towards the catcher the better. It gives her more time to see the ball, and also shrinks the strike zone. Of course, if the pitcher is throwing a lot of low pitches, the batter has to move forward (closer to the pitcher), to meet the ball before it drops. The feet should be close enough to the plate so that the end of the bat covers the outside portion of the plate with a few inches to spare.

3. The right foot should be set even with the left, or preferably a few inches back, behind the batter; the left or front foot closer to the plate. The back foot should be pointed straight ahead, or pigeon-toed a bit for more power.

4. The weight should be on the balls of the toes, a bit more weight on the back foot. Sometimes I stick a glove or a bat under the right heel to keep the weight on the toes. Flat-footedness is a no-no; less power and control, it causes a jerky swing.

5. Bend the knees a bit, as much as is comfortable. The idea is to be loose, to have the feeling of balance.

6. Likewise for the waist, bend forward a little bit. It helps the batter loosen up, keeps the weight forward on the balls of the toes, and gets the head closer to the strike zone to see the ball.

7. The hands should be together, an inch or so from the bottom of the bat. Make sure the bat is not too heavy. The guys in the pros today have gotten away from the big heavy bats used in

Figure 1
THE STANCE — FRONT VIEW

Figure 2
THE STANCE — SIDE VIEW

the old days. The bats are still big, but the grips are thinned out. This allows them to whip the bat head around very quickly. Bat speed is important, so have your child start off with a light bat. It's possible, however, to have too light a bat. In 1989 I had a kid named Danny, big kid, who was having trouble making contact. His dad was helping me coach, and I told him it was mechanical. One day at pre-game batting practice, I told Danny to get a heavier bat. Then he started making contact! During the game he smashed a screaming double, went two for three, and won the game. So, sometimes you have to experiment. Also, choke up a few inches if needed to be in complete control of the bat. Don't interlock fingers, even if the golfer in your family thinks it's a good idea.

8. The grip, holding the bat, should be firm, not quite a squeeze, but nice and firm. Tell your child to "feel" the strength in her wrist and forearm through the hands into the bat. There are different ways to place the hands in relation to each other. If the big sections of the fingers on both hands are in a line, this

Figure 3
CHOKE-UP & GRIP

Open grip: control

Tight grip: power

tends to give a bit more control, relying more on the wrist. If they are directly above or below the knuckles of the other hand this tighter grip gives more power, drawing in forearms and shoulders. Start with lining the knuckles up. (See Figure 3.)

9. The hands should be kept up by the right shoulder, not lower than the top of the strike zone. I like to see the hands right in front of or just behind the right shoulder, about six inches out. Holding the bat too low is a part of the stance you must change — no choice, hands have to be up.

10. The bat should point up and back a bit towards the catcher. Make sure it's not wrapped back behind the head, no need for the top of the bat to travel farther than necessary. Some kids like to wrap it around their head, or sit it on the shoulder; they must change this.

11. The right elbow should be up, away from the body, not so high as to be uncomfortable. This is important. A lot of kids will start the swing with that back elbow and the upper arm too close to the body. This can cause the whole right side to drop, causing a golf-like uppercut swing, one of the more difficult problems to cure. Stop it early! The swing must be level, and one key to a level swing is hand and elbow position. The elbow keeps the shoulders level. A level swing has a much better chance of hitting the ball. This is one of the keys, and it must be emphasized. You want to make sure that the angle between the upper arm and the right side of the chest is at least 45 degrees, and closer to 90 degrees, almost straight out.

12. The head should obviously be looking at the pitcher, chin tucked in near the left shoulder. The left shoulder is tucked in a bit towards the plate. The eyes are focused on the spot where the pitcher will release the ball, at the top of his stretch. It's important to keep the head stationary (just like in golf).

13. Now the stance is ready. One more thing, the body must be still. No unnecessary motion that could cause the bat to move a millimeter from the spot where the eyes say the ball is. It also helps concentration. Some guys like to "dance," move their feet around, or shake the bat. It may help their nerves, but it never helps the swing. Be still. Like a coiled snake, like a cat on its haunches, like a guided missile, waiting, ready to explode on the

Figure 4
IMPROPER STANCES

Not sideways

Hands too low

Bat wrapped around head

Too far past plate

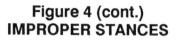

Figure 4 (cont.)
IMPROPER STANCES

Stiff legged

Shoulders not level

Over-rotated, back to pitcher

Weight too far forward

Figure 4 (cont.)
IMPROPER STANCES

Feet too close

Hands too close to body

Too close to plate

Hands not together

ball in one sharp, quick motion. Talk about these concepts as you work with your child. Tell her to stay balanced. We want her thinking about these things, not how well she is doing. We want to get her mind off herself and onto the ball. Remember, be still but not stiff!

The Swing

We have talked about the initial part of the swing, such as keeping the eye on the ball all the way to the bat, keeping loose and still, leaning forward and keeping the weight back especially on the balls of the toes of the back foot, keeping the bat pointed up and back a bit, keeping the wrists and forearms strong, and holding the bat firmly, right elbow away from the body, hands up. Now we will discuss the swing itself.

1. Get a good pitch. Another reason to keep your eye on the ball is so you can pick out a good pitch. This is a very important fundamental. A ball out of the strike zone cannot be hit well, and cannot be hit hard. High pitches pop up, low ones turn into weak grounders. Inside or outside pitches are usually hit foul. Most of the time it's a swinging strike. Tell your child to look for the good pitch, never let a good pitch go by because you don't get that many. When you pitch, talk about each pitch — was it a ball or a strike? In practice it's okay to swing at bad pitches (if they are at least close!) because it teaches bat control, but make sure your child knows when the pitch is not in the strike zone. He will, eventually, be able to tell the difference before the ball is halfway to him. Talk about these concepts.

2. Step into the pitch. The biggest fear kids have in batting is getting hit by the ball. (The second is fear of embarrassing themselves.) So a major problem with a lot of kids is what we call "stepping into the bucket"! (See Figure 5.) They step away from the ball, towards third base, as they swing. This causes their body, and consequently the bat, to move out of the strike zone. No way they can hit anything except maybe an inside pitch.

This part of the swing is called the stride; it is a short six to eight inch step towards the pitcher. The idea here is to get the body moving directly towards the pitcher, into the ball. The stride is preceded by shifting or rocking the weight further to the back

Figure 5
STEP INTO THE PITCH

Proper swing — step forward   *Improper swing — stepping into the bucket*

foot. Keep the weight back as long as possible to prevent striding too soon. Now your child is ready to begin the swing, a quick, powerful, balanced, exploding action. He must drive or push himself forward with the back foot, and lift or step the front foot towards the pitcher. The back foot pivots, allowing first the hips and ultimately the whole upper torso to turn. The front foot does not point towards the pitcher, but just slides forward. I remember a husky, freckle-faced redhead named Todd, who as a ten year old had a bad habit of stepping out. His dad said he had been doing it for two years. He was a good hitter, except he usually couldn't reach the ball after stepping back so far. So he struck out a lot. I had his father put a cinderblock behind both feet in practice, and it worked. It took a while, but he settled down and started to become the hitter he was.

Some kids don't stride at all. Their swing is stiff and jerky, so it is very hard to hit the ball squarely. One way to deal with this is to have them take practice swings, without a pitched ball. Just step and swing, about fifty times a day. Tell them to pretend they see the ball coming towards them, and step into the pitch and swing! It will loosen up their swing. Don't let them get sloppy. Do about twenty-five at first and build up to fifty quality swings. If it gets to be a habit, then they will do it naturally in a real situation. We used to get a bat in the living room, and take some swings, talking about the stance and the swing. Try it (but just move the lamps out of the way).

Remember, the concept here is to get the body moving with the swing into the ball, and to avoid stepping away from the ball.

3. Swing level. I remember I had a nine year old one year named Keith. He loved to play ball, and did it with his heart. But he had the worst swing I ever saw. It looked like he was hitting a golf ball out of a sand trap, a wild looping uppercut. First of all, if he hit the ball it went straight up. Second, he missed a lot because such a swing requires more timing. The bat is moving upward and has to meet the ball at a single spot. A level swing can meet the ball anywhere over the plate. Third, such a swing causes the shoulders to tilt severely, and this moves the head up and takes the eyes off the ball.

I tried everything with Keith. I had him hold his hands higher, and get his right elbow up more. I told him to try to chop down at the ball, like chopping a tree down. (By the way, these suggestions often do work, and you should always try them first.) Finally, I had no choice but to tell him to bat lefty. Kids usually will swing level from the opposite side, albeit with less power. He still hit the ball well. The next year, his coach moved him back to righty — and time had softened the arc in his swing. Some things just need time. Keith will make the all-star team someday, but it's too bad that his bad habit, developed very young, held him back a few years.

The way to teach your child to swing level is to tell him to straighten out his left arm and move his hands directly towards the ball, on a straight line. We would rather perceive the bat coming down to meet the ball rather than up into it. The bat will then also move on a straight line. (See Figure 6.) As noted earlier, holding the hands up and keeping the shoulders level (don't drop the right side) are also helpful to a level swing. Another

Figure 6
SWING

Proper swing — level

Improper uppercut swing — batter drops right side and lifts head

Lunge — reaching for the ball too soon

Step into bucket

cause of an uppercut swing is lifting up the head. If this occurs, remind your child to keep the head down and still.

4. Another key to a level swing is to make sure that the player doesn't "hitch." A hitch is a cocking motion that many players make with their hands just as they go into their swing. They move their hands down and up, instead of keeping them still and moving them straight out towards the ball. A hitch also takes time and will cause a player to swing late at a fastball. Tell her to keep her hands still, and move them outward only with the swing, directly at the ball. A backward hitch is better than an up and down one, but no hitch is best of all.

5. Open the hips. As noted earlier, we want to keep the weight back and hips steady as long as possible. Then, just at the end of the stride and beginning of the swing, the hips turn or "open up" giving power, speed, and torque to the swing. We want the hips ultimately to open up completely, facing the pitcher. (See Figure 7.)

6. Extend the arms. A tight swing, hands close to the chest, choppy, often goes along with stepping into the bucket. It's a defensive swing. Such a swing may indicate some self-doubt or concern about getting hit by the ball. It also is often found with a stance which puts the weight back on the heels, standing straight up instead of leaning forward at the knees and waist. One way to deal with it is to have the player stand farther from the plate during practice, to force him to bend forward, weight forward, and extend the arms fully at the point of contact. Tell him to "throw his hands out at the ball," and this will extend the arms.

Hit through the ball. Some kids just chop or slap at the ball. The idea is to hit through the ball. They need to follow through with the swing, so the bat ends up all the way behind them. Try to hold the head down as long as possible, and keep the back foot down, on the toes, but not dragging.

Figure 7
OPEN THE HIPS

Hips fully open

Hips stiff, partially open

SUMMARY AND OTHER TIPS

If you have read this far, you know as much as you need to about hitting in order to help your son or daughter. Let's summarize, and if this seems repetitious, then I'm practicing what I preach, I'll do a lot of repetition in this book.

Be supportive generally — if you can't drive him to practice help him find some way to get there, make a phone call to another parent.

Be positive. She is a hitter already, she just has to believe that. Don't help her confirm her doubts about herself.

Promote repetition. Go out and pitch to him, or have a catch. If there are a few kids around, suggest they play ball. Get them organized into a game, help oversee it, pitch to them. Sometimes kids will argue for two hours about who is on what team, or who is up first. You can get them beyond that, get them on their way to doing it. When I pitch to my son Joey, I grab a bucket of balls and it takes only about ten or fifteen minutes to get thirty to forty swings. We go pick up the balls together.

It's important to practice, very important. Don't forget a fifteen minute workout will make brownie points with your own body too, and we all could use more exercise.

Finally, the basics: learn what to look for in a stance. Look at the placement of the feet, the knees, the hands. Is he standing too stiffly? Bend knees and waist to loosen up. Look at the swing, is it level? Is he dropping his shoulder, elbow, hands, whole right side? Does he see the ball the whole way to the bat?

Don't push too hard, don't berate him if he doesn't feel like playing, just suggest it. Once he starts to improve, and he definitely will improve with your help, his desire to play will soar. Kids love to do something they feel good about. They love to have fun.

Here's another of my secrets, maybe my best one! When I pitched to my kids, Jackie, Sis, and Joey, I did so while down on my right knee. I've been doing it this way for fifteen years, since Jackie was four. I remember when I was a kid, my coach always seemed so tall, and the ball would be coming down on me from eight feet high. It was dropping fast, and I had to swing an uppercut to get a solid contact. When you pitch on a knee, the ball leaves your hand the same height that a ten year old's does. It comes at your son or daughter in a much more level flight.

Now pitching from the knee sounds tough, and I guess it is, but I didn't notice. If your son is young, and you do it from thirty-five to forty feet, you can develop some control. It will come! You have to have faith in practice if you are going to teach its value to someone else. If your son is big, eleven or twelve, don't get closer than forty feet or you might wind up wearing the ball. By the way, you don't need a catcher, and don't let your wife or someone get back there without a face mask and other protection. A foul tip is hard to catch, and may hit the face. You'll get used to the strike zone. If you have several balls, use them all, then go pick them up when you are out. This also helps to get a lot of swings in a short period of time. I use about ten or fifteen balls. I get them as a coach, you build up a supply. I buy a box (twelve) each year for myself. If your kid is under ten, the ninety-nine cent cork balls are good enough. I've seen them on sale for seventy-nine cents. Older kids bang them out of shape too quickly.

ONE MORE TIP: get something soft to kneel on, it makes it easier to be able to walk after practice. I use a catcher's chest protector. A small pillow is okay.

I think pitching on my knee has resulted in quality batting practice. Of all my secrets, I think this is the most effective. I'll tell you, my teams always hit the ball, so something is working.

There are two other drills that are good for parents, and will save having to chase balls. Your local sporting goods store will have a "ball on a string" which you whip around your head in a circular motion and then step towards your child, moving the ball into the strike zone. This is excellent practice. Another drill is to stand to the side and lob the ball into the strike zone. Your son can stand facing the backstop (or a net), so the ball doesn't go far.

Batting tees are used in some of the pre-Little League clinics. I have mixed feelings about them. They teach a kid to swing differently a bit, since they don't need to worry about timing to meet a moving ball. Yet it does get the kids involved at a very young age — six or seven — and you are pretty much guaranteed to hit the ball. So it's also a positive thing. I always pitched to my kids, underhand if I had to, but the ball was moving. Try it if you want, maybe combine it with pitching, depending on the age of your children.

Have you ever heard of pepper? It's an exercise they do in the big leagues where a coach will stand six feet from a couple of players and softly hit them grounders. They lob the ball back to the bat and he hits to someone else; you keep it moving and it develops reflexes. I do the reverse for batting. I get the kids up close with bats and they try to hit it softly to where I tell them — at my shoe, my knee, my glove. It's a great drill, it builds confidence and a sense of contact with the ball! Try it with your son or daughter, just a few minutes each time.

A few words about equipment are in order. Little League starts in the spring, and it's often cold. The season starts early because vacations often begin right after school and, invariably, some kids will leave then. Also, tournaments start at that time and the better players go to all-star teams. When it's cold, the bat stings the hands when it hits the ball. A batting glove will eliminate the sting. Get one for each hand, a cheap one will do. If his winter gloves are not too thick, they will work, too. Even a pair of socks are better than nothing, although they will make the bat a bit slippery and harder to hold onto. You probably won't be throwing hard enough to need a helmet, but it never hurts. Any hard hat or helmet will do. Spikes help to give traction to the right foot as it drives the body towards the ball, but they are not essential for practice. Remember, use a light bat, don't fall into the trap of getting something so heavy it warps the swing.

SWITCH HITTING

Well, not too many kids can do it. I guess it's tough enough to get good from one side. But when you watch the pros, half the team is platooned — righties facing lefties, and vice versa. The idea is that a righty can see the ball better if it comes from the pitcher's left side (batter's right side). It starts out in front of the batter. Whereas when the pitcher's lefty, especially sidearm lefty, the ball seems like it's starting from behind the batter. I really can't say I've emphasized switch hitting. I do have my kids bat lefty a few pitches at practices, just so they can see what it feels like. I should do more of it. I basically use the left stance to change something a player is doing wrong.

I remember when I was about nine or ten. We had just moved to the country, and I had never played baseball. I joined a team and couldn't hit the ball to save my life. Then one day after what seemed like a million strike-outs, my coach told me to get up lefty. I don't know whether he had an idea, or was just frustrated. But I got a hit the first time up. The new angle forced me to look at the ball better, somehow I saw it better (because the pitcher was righty?). I also swung more level. It felt awkward, and I had less power, but it worked. I'll never forget the cheer I got when I was out there on first base.

Figure 8
BUNTING

BUNTING

Bunting is a lost art in youth baseball. Very few coaches teach it — but I like to do some of it. I guess it's because the pitcher is so close to the batter (only forty-six feet instead of sixty feet, six inches as in the pros), that he can get to the ball very quickly and throw the batter out. Nevertheless, it should be practiced.

I remember a playoff game in 1986, nine year olds, and we needed a run to tie the score. We were facing a kid named Keith, the best pitcher in the league. He threw hard, and he threw strikes. The boy who was up could make contact, but he was small and couldn't get the ball out of the infield, not against Keith. The on-deck batter (the next batter up) was a very good hitter. So I told the batter to bunt, and run like the dickens. It worked. He got on and my next batter tied the game with a shot in the gap.

When practicing bunting, tell the batters to turn and face the pitcher just as he pitches the ball. (See Figure 8.) He should slide his right hand a third of the way towards the top. Keep the head of the bat high in the strike zone, you want to hit down on the ball. He's got to concentrate on the ball more closely, watch its spin. Then let the ball hit the bat. If he moves the bat towards the ball it will roll right to the pitcher, so just hold the bat firmly and let the ball hit the bat, even pull the head of the bat back a bit. Tell your child to try to hit it down the third base line softly, and be running as he does. Foot speed helps here — don't look back, just go for the base.

Well, that's it for hitting. It's all you need, more than you need. You can stop here and still be a great help, because hitting is of primary importance. However, if you want your child to be really good at the other things he does while he is waiting to bat, then read on!

2.

FIELDING

To many ballplayers, defense is just "de thing you try to hit de ball over." Unfortunately, this is why defense is often the last thing kids learn. Some coaches completely ignore it, except as regards their better athletes. The rest of the kids they just stick out in the outfield to stand around. They figure a kid either has it or he doesn't.

As a result, a typical youth baseball scenario starts with an error, and soon players are throwing the ball all over the place. Scores are high with the younger kids because of poor defense.

Part of the problem is that there is usually not enough practice time in youth baseball. You get the kids for only a few hours a week. During the season the fields are often reserved for games, so there is very little practice opportunity. That's where we parents come in. There are some simple things you can teach your child, and there can be substantial improvement in defensive play with some regular practice.

Fielding is essentially catching and throwing. We'll address both skills generally. Chapter 5 will discuss defense further from the perspective of each individual field position.

CATCHING

The best way to begin learning how to catch is to do just that, have a catch. Get a couple of gloves and a ball, and go out and throw it softly back and forth. Start at a comfortable distance — fifteen to twenty-five feet. I've seen a lot of parents, especially mothers who have had little experience with baseball, learn very quickly. Remember, if you practice, you will improve too, so don't be bashful. It may be easier to use a tennis ball at first, or a rubber ball. Usually a five-and-ten cent store will have a rubber ball filled with a sponge-like material. These are preferable because they weigh a bit more, behaving like a hard ball in flight, but do not hurt if they hit you. I frequently use a rubber ball when I have outfield practice, especially for players who are having trouble catching. Go to a hard ball for short catches as soon as you can.

Remember, a key to confidence is not pushing too hard. Start from a position that allows you both to do well, and gradually increase the difficulty when you are both ready. Recognize and celebrate improvement! If you start with too difficult a distance, your child will not be able to handle it, and will only learn to fail. If it's not working, make it easier. A challenge is okay, but an impossible challenge is negative.

Catching Fly Balls

The main idea in catching pop-ups is to get under the ball so it's traveling right at the head. I know this sounds strange, but it's the best way to catch. It's just like hitting: you must keep your eye on the ball, and you can see it best when it's coming right at your eyes. The glove should above the head when the ball is caught.

Many kids are afraid to try this for obvious reasons, especially if they have already gotten hit by the ball. So they let the ball fall to one side of them, and try to catch it at the waist. The trouble with such a catch is they have to calculate two more angles, and it's much easier to misjudge it. (See Figure 9.) If the ball is coming right at the eye, all she has to do is stick her glove in the way at the right time. Now, this is why I use rubber or tennis

Figure 9
CATCHING POP-UPS

Proper position — directly under the ball   *Improper position — allowing ball to drop to one side*

balls for the younger ages. Just tell your son or daughter to drop back to a short outfield distance, and throw the ball high. They will know it won't hurt since it's rubber, and will try harder to get under it. Take it slow, start with a short distance if you need to and, over a few weeks, work out to a longer distance. Make sure the sun is not in their eyes, so pick an appropriate angle from the sun. Build confidence slowly. It may take a very long time, so just relax and be patient.

Kids usually misjudge fly balls by coming in too far, and letting the ball go over their heads. So when your child shows that she is able to catch the ball, start to vary the distance. First throw over her head. Then throw one short, then to the right or left. On throws to the right of the fielder, she will have to turn her glove backward (see Figure 10) and catch it backhanded. On throws over her head, tell her to turn and run. Do not run backward! She will get to the ball faster, and be able to make a more relaxed

Figure 10
CHASING DOWN POP-UPS

Back handing ball to side oppo-
site glove

Running back to catch a deep fly
ball

catch. As noted earlier, if the ball goes directly to the fielder, she catches the ball above her head, with her fingers up and palm facing the sky.

Remind her to try to catch the ball in the webbing of the glove — it reduces the chance that the ball will pop-out, and it avoids stinging the palm of the hand. Also, tell her to use both hands. The free hand stays by the glove and smothers the ball when it hits the glove. This accomplishes two things: it keeps the ball from popping out of the glove, and it gets the ball into her throwing hand faster so she wastes no time getting the ball back to the infield.

Fungo practice, as it is called, involves a coach hitting the ball to the fielders. It takes some skill to do. That's why fungo bats are extra big. I find it easier to throw the ball, you will too! Don't throw your arm out. Always warm up first with a dozen or so short throws, then go for some longer ones. Just get a dozen or so long ones in and that's all your child will need at each session.

Moreover, it's good to move to different drills, just a few minutes on each. Variety keeps everyone more interested. Focus on different skills each day.

It may be that your child will miss nearly every catch at first. "No problem," tell him, "tomorrow or the next day we'll catch one or two. Then after that more and more." Focus on slight improvement. Don't set expectations too high. Don't get frustrated — your son will sense your frustration and feel it too. After a while, he will improve.

Catching Grounders

Catching infield grounders is tougher. It's the toughest thing in youth baseball. Again, some people figure that you either have it or you don't. It takes a keen, quick reflex, speed, and good concentration to be an infielder. Okay, so everybody won't be able to play everywhere, no problem. Eye-hand coordination varies for kids. It can be tested. I am not an infielder, I just never had the range. In any event, give your child a shot at it.

The first thing is to find a smooth surface. Most grass fields are terrible. They only teach a kid to fear grounders since a bad hop occurs very frequently. A dirt field is much better, and you can rake out any ruts and remove stones. I once took my son into a parking lot. Use a side street if traffic is very light. Throw the ball to him sidearm, or somehow make sure you release it about two feet from the ground at the height where a bat would hit it. At first let him stand fairly close and throw the ball softly, get it to him on one bounce. Again, throwing it works as well as hitting it, and takes less skill on your part. Also, you can put the ball exactly where you want it. After a while, when he can handle it, make it tougher. Give a couple of bounces, vary the speed, throw to the right or left. As in the outfield, the fielder reverses her glove position on shots to the side opposite the glove hand, catching it backhanded.

As with outfielding, the idea is to get in front of the ball so it's coming right at you. Catch the ball to the side only if you must in order to reach it. The player stands in a crouch, facing the batter, legs spread out a bit, hands and gloves down by the knees, weight forward on the toes so he can spring one way or the other. When the ball is hit, the player springs, not steps but springs, to get quickly to the spot where he can make the play.

I used to tell my players that infielders have to "stand up and sit down at the same time." The legs are spread apart, left foot up, right foot back. The knees are bent so his backside is down low. (Not really sitting of course, but it makes the point. We want the body low.) Most players prefer to bend over at the waist, and a slight waist bend is needed but not at the expense of bending the knees. We don't want the head down too far. "Bend from the knee, not from the waist." Repeat this sentence constantly. (See Figure 11.)

Finally, the glove is down, way down. "Come up with some dirt on it," I always say. If the ball goes under the glove, it's all over. Start the glove low, and bring it forward and up to meet the ball. Visualize a triangle with the glove and both feet. Players often expect the ball to bounce up to them, but sometimes it doesn't. If it was hit on the top of the ball, the topspin will make it skim the ground. The glove must always be low in anticipation of this.

Another popular tip is to tell your child to visualize a funnel with the open mouth receiving the ball and channeling it to the waist. The key here is that the hands must be soft, giving way to the ball. The scooping action therefore brings the glove forward to the ball, then gently back to the waist.

Tell her that it's important not to stand back on the heels, just waiting for the ball to play you. A fielder must play the ball. If it's slow, run in to get it, otherwise get in front and scoop it up. The forward action is the aggressiveness needed to command the ball. Again, if you practice on a smooth surface, these skills will be much easier to demonstrate and learn.

The biggest problems with kids catching grounders are 1) not getting in front of the ball; 2) not getting the glove low enough (not bending the knees enough) and; 3) coming up too soon, especially with the head.

I had an all-star first baseman in 1987, a ten year old named Chris. He could hit the ball a mile, but his fielding was not consistent. One day before regular practice, he and his father got there early to practice grounders. He had made some errors the previous game, and I was worried a bit. I guess they were too! I

Figure 11
FIELDING GROUNDERS

Proper stance as ball is pitched

Spring to get in front of ball

*Stand up and sit down: get low,
bend knees, and lower glove*

*Keep head down and scoop the
ball up and back to the waist*

watched him closely, focusing on different parts of the body. After several plays I saw it! Just as the ball was about to be caught, he would lift his head up, and up would go the shoulders, the arms and, of course, the glove. It's understandable. Kids are worried about the ball getting a bad hop into the face, so they lift or turn their heads. I told Chris about it, and then kept saying "stay down, stay down, stay calm" as the ball approached him. It took a while, but he started to adjust. If he keeps working at it, he will eliminate the problem permanently.

Reflexes are important in infield play. So you practice them. I used to get two balls and stand about twenty feet from my son. I would throw one, and throw another just as he was releasing the ball back to me. Quick, to the left, to the right, change speeds. Quick. It improves the reflexes. That's another drill you can do for a few minutes.

Remember, as with hitting, don't be impatient with the misses, the booted balls, the errors. They happen even to the pros. Reward the catches with a smile, or "way to go." And,

Figure 12
DRILL FOR FIELDING GROUNDERS

Set up cones as goal posts and have child try to stop grounders

repeat, repeat, repeat! Repetition is the backbone of success and improvement. The more the better. Make it fun. Put up two empty bottles a short distance to the left and right of her, like a soccer goal, and see how many grounders she can stop. Keep score, have a goal. Increase it over time. Tell her constantly to keep her eye on the ball. (See Figure 12.)

The Glove

A few words are in order about the glove, and this may be the most important thing about catching. Your child needs a decent glove, and it must be broken in. It is nearly impossible to catch a ball with the cheap, rigid, plastic junk you find in a toy store. The ball will just jump out every time. Even for a good glove it takes a year to break it in, soften it up.

When I get a new glove, I literally beat it up. Rub glove oil onto it, and bend every inch of it back and forth. Keep bending the fingers back and forth, hit it with a bat, jump on it. Years ago they used to drop it in a pail of water and hang it out to dry (I've never tried it). Suffice it to say, the glove should be soft, so it collapses on the ball. I've seen so many kids get a negative picture of their ability because of the quickie-cheap gloves they got.

Leave a ball in the pocket when you are done practicing, and wrap the glove around it. I usually wrapped the glove in a winter scarf, at least until my wife made me stop.

THROWING

There is really not a whole lot I can tell you about throwing, pitching yes, but throwing no. But there is a lot you can do about it. Throwing is almost totally dependent on just doing it. Your son needs to throw a ball a few thousand times before he gets the smooth style of a decent throw. So go and have a catch with him or her. Having a catch is a great American pastime. It's something you can do anywhere, anytime. However, at early ages, it is critical to developing a good throw.

Start nice and easy, fifteen to twenty-five feet apart, and slowly move back to sixty feet. The more times he throws the ball, the faster and better his arm will work out the coordination needed. It will come. You really can't teach throwing, you just have to do it.

Throwing Basics

Of course, there are a few basics you can look for. Last year I had a girl named Suzanne on my team, a good athlete, but she had never seen a baseball. Everybody throws awkwardly when they are just starting — like I say, it takes a thousand or so tosses to begin developing a smooth throw. Try throwing lefty a few times, and you will know how a beginner feels.

Anyway, I looked at her carefully. And, I repeat, to be a coaching parent you must force yourself to focus on different parts of the body, to find things they are doing wrong. I looked at her foot position and saw that she was throwing off her left foot,

Figure 13
THROWING FORM

Proper form. Pushing off same foot as throwing arm (right arm, right foot) NOTE: full arm extension, shoulder points to target

Improper form. Pushing off with opposite foot and arm (left foot, right arm)

that is, she was pushing off her left foot and stepping forward with her right foot — it was backwards! The idea in throwing (for righties) is to push off on the right foot as you begin the throw, and step or land on the left as you release the throw. (See Figure 13.) I also tell my players always to get set before they throw, plant the back foot, and get off a good throw. Sometimes there is no time, and you have to throw off balance or on the run. That's when a lot of throwing errors are made.

Another tip about throwing is to reach back with the ball and then after you cock the arm and wrist to throw, extend the arm. A lot of kids are arm-throwers. They bend their elbow too much and throw entirely with their arm — it looks like they are literally "throwing the arm" instead of the ball. When the arm is extended, the shoulder becomes the fulcrum and brings the strength of the entire body into the throw. The hands and arm move in a circular motion. The elbow-bent arm-thrower cuts off the power coming from the right leg, right hip, and right shoulder. He gets less power on the throw, and his arm will quickly tire since it is doing all the work. Remember to keep the elbow high — at or over the shoulder.

GRIP — Grip on the ball is pretty standard — thumb on bottom, the next two fingers (index and middle) on top, the last two fingers tucked on the right. If your son's hand is small, let him use the three middle fingers on top, with only the pinky tucked on the right side. Fingers can straddle or cross the seams, but in a fielding play he won't have time to worry about seams. (See Figure 14.) Also, make sure the ball is not set back in the hand too far, against the palm. There should be some space there. The idea is to throw with the fingers.

AIM — The left or non-throwing shoulder and the left foot both point in the direction of the target. Eyes must look right at the target. Some kids like to throw the ball high in a big soft arc. I think it's because they feel they control it better, maybe it's because it's easier. Anyway, a throw should always be as hard and level as possible, a line drive. A ball thrown straight on a line is called a "rope," this means it was thrown straight, like a rope clothesline. I always tell my players to throw right at the guy's chest or head. That is the best height for them to catch the ball, so that's where we want to throw it.

Figure 14
GRIPPING THE BALL

Proper grip. If the hand is small, all three middle fingers may be placed on top

Ball not set too deeply into hand

For infielders, as I noted earlier, the key is to get the ball out of the glove as quickly as possible. The throwing hand should go for the ball at the moment it hits the glove, and make the transition very quickly. We'll discuss this again in Chapter 5.

VELOCITY — The velocity of the throw depends on where you are playing. A third baseman or shortstop really has to rifle the ball to get it to first base. However, the second baseman needs only to ensure a firm throw to first base. If she throws too hard she risks a control problem, throwing the ball away, and it's much harder for the first baseman to catch. This goes also for the pitcher, when he throws to first. The shortstop will make a soft throw to second base on a ball hit to her left side with a man on first. Field the ball, turn to the bag, and just lob the ball, underhanded if she is very close to the second baseman. This also happens on grounders to the first baseman. She softly tosses the ball to the pitcher covering first base, if necessary. Run to the base if possible, but throw to the pitcher if needed.

An outfielder on the other hand always throws hard. The key to his throw is to get rid of the ball quickly. How many times do we see the outfielders stand there holding the ball while runners are flying around the bases?

Of course, the problem with such an outfielder is that he doesn't know where to throw the ball. He has to think about it, take a look at the runners, decide where to throw. He sees a lot of commotion in the infield, he is excited because he just caught the ball, and he doesn't know what to do. So the runners run, and the parents scream, and the poor kid gets so nervous he throws the ball into the parking lot.

THE CUT-OFF AND THROWING AHEAD OF THE LEAD RUNNER

Outfielders are always supposed to hit the cut-off man. If the ball is hit to left field, or the left of centerfield, the shortstop is usually the cut-off. If it's to the right side, the second baseman usually gets it. However, with men on base, the cut-off concept becomes a bit more complicated.

Since this book is for parents, you may wonder whether we really need to go into detail on the concept of the cut-off but, unfortunately, other than what I said above, about the usual cut-off responsibility of the shortstop and second baseman, many coaches don't know anything else. Some just say "always throw the ball to second base." Well, I agree that it's better than nothing, better than holding the ball. But it's not baseball. It's not defense. And if the coach doesn't understand the concept, he obviously can't teach it to your child. So you can do it instead. It's really very logical, common sense stuff. I recommend you learn it and then talk about the concepts on a drive to Grandma's house — that's how I did it.

The concept of the cut-off is based on the attempt to stop the lead runner. The lead runner is the one who is closest to scoring. If there are men on first and second bases, the man on second is the lead runner. If there is only a man on first, then he is the lead runner. He is the man we want to stop. The way to stop him is to throw to the base ahead of him. An important defensive concept, perhaps the most important one, is throwing ahead of the lead runner. It's very simple, you just have to know where the lead runner is and throw towards the base in front of him.

Now, on a single to the outfield. A lead runner on first will get to second easily. We want to stop him from going to third base, so that's where we throw it, towards third base. Since he will be on second base by the time the outfielder gets the ball, then the base ahead of him is third base. If the play starts with a man on second, he will go to third easily on a single to the outfield, so the base in front of him is home plate. This is complicated, that's why many coaches don't understand it. Just read it a few times.

But while we focus on the lead runner, we also want to be able to stop the batter from going to second base, if the need occurs. If the outfielder throws to third base or home, the batter will have time to advance. So in order to get ourselves in position to have a play on both the lead runner and the batter, we position a fielder called a cut-off. If the lead runner was on first, the cut-off stands in the path of the ball about twenty feet before third base. This player has the option of letting the ball proceed to third base to get the lead runner, or cutting it off to make a play on the batter. He may, for instance, feel that there is a better chance to get the batter out if he is running to second base. Or, if the ball is thrown off-line and will not get to the third baseman, then the ball should automatically be cut off. In this instance the cut-off is just trying to keep control of the ball, and not let a bad throw go into foul territory.

So the cut-off player needs to line up between the outfielder and third base. With a man on first, I like the shortstop always to be the cut-off. (See Figure 15.) If the ball is coming from right field, the shortstop can best determine whether to let the ball go through to the third baseman, or to cut it off. If the lead runner stopped at second, she cuts it off anyway. If the runner will make it to third in her judgment (and then the third baseman must tell her what to do), she cuts it off to keep the guy who hit the ball from going to second base. Read this a few times. Once you have the concept in mind, you will automatically know what to do. It's

Figure 15
CUT-OFF PLAY WITH LEAD RUNNER ON FIRST

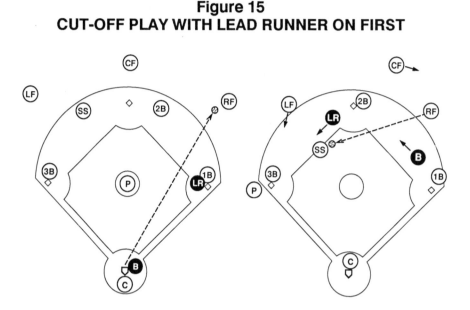

Start of play. Ball hit to right field. Lead runner (LR) on first

Proper position. Right fielder throws toward third base in front of lead runner. Shortstop is cut-off to hold batter at first

not a matter of memorizing what to do, it's a principle that says simply stop the lead runner by throwing ahead of him, and give yourself a shot at other runners by hitting the cut-off.

Suppose there is a man on second. Then he is the lead runner. We want to stop him from going home on a single. So the outfielder throws ahead of the lead runner; she throws home. For this play the cut-off is the pitcher. The pitcher is the closest player to home. If there is a play at the plate, the pitcher first looks at the ball to see if it was thrown straight. If not, she will probably have to cut it off, since they will not get the man at the plate anyway, and she needs to make sure the other runners don't advance. Now, I know I'll catch some flak here, because in big league play the pitcher backs up third or home and, depending on which side the ball was hit to, the third baseman or first

Figure 16
CUT-OFF PLAY WITH LEAD RUNNER ON SECOND

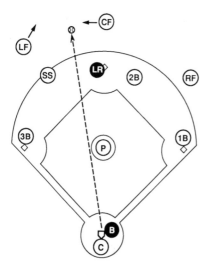

Start of play. Ball hit to center-field. LR on second base

Proper position. Centerfielder throws ahead of lead runner toward home. Pitcher is cut-off to hold batter at first

baseman is the cut-off. Well, Little League fields are smaller, and I like the pitcher in the middle. (See Figure 16.)

Now, if there is no one on base at all then the batter is the lead runner. That's when we throw to second base, ahead of the batter, the lead runner. So the adage we always hear at Little League games about throwing to second base is only correct when there is no one else on base. In this case, as noted earlier, the cut-off is the shortstop or second baseman, depending on where the ball was hit. In Little League play the distance is so short that the outfielders are often very close to second base when they field the ball. So I just tell the cut-off man to stand on the base, and the other fielder backs him up. A cut-off only goes out to the fielder when it is needed. It depends on the distance and the strength of the fielder's throw. Nothing is automatic, that's why it's best for the kids to learn the concepts behind what they need to do. Then they can figure out what to do in a given play. I adjust things based on the abilities of fielders.

If there is a man on third, forget him. We never worry about a man on third on a ball hit safely to the outfield. He will always score. Outfielders only worry about a man on first or second. The only time a man on third comes into the picture is on a fly ball, when the runner will tag up and try to go home.

So there it is, that's what the cut-off is about. It's logical, and really very simple when you think about it. The purpose of defense is to stop runs from being scored. The outfielders therefore try to get the ball in front of the lead runner. They direct the ball to the next base to which this lead runner would go. If there is a play on that runner, a chance to get her, the ball is allowed to go through. If there is no play, the cut-off fielder catches the ball to see if he can make a play on the other runners, to stop them from advancing.

Of course, when the ball goes past the outfielder, to the fence, the strategy is the same, but the second baseman or shortstop has to go out to get the relay. Children can't throw the ball to the plate from 200 feet, at least not many. So the cut-off goes out to get the relay and then turns to see if there is a play. The pitcher or some other designated defensive leader can help by telling the cut-off where to throw the ball. On a ball hit to the fence, anyone on second or third base will score. The only hope is to stop the man on first (if there was one) from going home, or to catch the batter going to second base (if he is slow) or to third base. Since these are the only plays possible, you focus on them and ignore the rest.

RUNDOWNS

It often happens that a runner is caught between two bases. This situation calls for a run-down. It's a simple play that is usually fouled up. Its elements are as follows.

1) Get the runner to fully commit himself. Whoever has the ball, usually an infielder, must understand that the runner will want to see where the ball is thrown, and then run in the opposite direction. Therefore, the fielder, if this happens, should charge

the runner, and get him to commit first.

2) If the runner tries to advance to the next base, get the ball quickly to that base. We always want to run the runner back to a prior base, and attempt the put-out there. This is so, because if the put-out fails, at least the runner will not have advanced. This is particularly important for obvious reasons, when the rundown is between third base and home plate.

3) The fielder with the ball should hold it high, feigning a throw while running hard on the inside of the base path. This will confuse the runner who is trying to anticipate the throw. A good faked throw may get the runner to stop, to change direction, allowing the fielder to tag her. A well-executed run-down should require only one throw to retire the runner.

4) The rest is "feel" — if the fielder can make the tag she does so, otherwise she throws to the base in time for that fielder to take the tag.

5) The fielder covering the base towards which the runner is heading should be off the base at least several feet towards the runner on the inside of the base path. This is so because if the throw is a bit late she still has time to make a tag. How many times do we see a runner slide under a late throw to a fielder standing on the bag? If you see a run-down in the pros, the receiving fielder is usually off the bag and calls for the throw when the runner is close. Note: If all fielders are slightly to the inside of the base path we will avoid hitting the runner with the ball.

6) Other available fielders who are not guarding another runner should back up the fielder involved in the run-down. They are often needed.

Okay, so that's what a parent needs to know generally about fielding. In fact, it's more than you need to know. The main things are to go and have a catch, use a rubber ball for outfield practice, throw the ball instead of batting it, urge him or her to get under a pop-up and down low and in front of the grounders. Talk about defensive dynamics, and the need to hit the cut-off while throwing in front of the lead runner. He'll improve, especially if you spend the time. Remember, a few minutes every other day is not much, but it can accomplish a great deal. Try it! It may come slowly for both of you, so be patient and enjoy the improvement as it comes.

3.
RULES OF THE GAME

FIELD DIMENSIONS AND GENERAL RULES

There is no need to go into great detail on rules. But there are some basics you should know. If you want more information, write to Little League Baseball, P.O. Box 3485, Williamsport, PA 17701, and ask for a copy of the official Little League rules. I'll also include a glossary of terms so you can start learning to speak the language of baseball.

Baseball is a game where players hit pitched balls onto a field of play, and then try to run past four bases, without being tagged, to score runs. The defense tries to get the player out before he scores. Each team has three outs in each of nine innings. An out is usually made when the batter gets three strikes, when a hit ball is caught before it touches the ground, when a runner is tagged between bases, or when a player with the ball touches a base which the runner must get to. A player must advance to first base when he hits a ball which touches the ground before being caught or when the pitcher misses the strike zone four times. Normally, the player may advance to second, third, and home base at his own risk, but he must advance if another hit ball touches the ground. Nine players are permitted to each team at one time.

Figure 17
REGULATION LITTLE LEAGUE FIELD

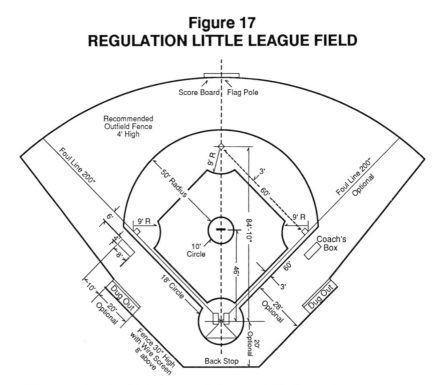

Diagram showing Little League field layout. All dimensions are compulsory unless marked "Optional"

A Little League field is small, compared to big league fields. Players up to twelve years old, inclusive, play on a field about 2/3 the size of a big league field. Little League bases are sixty feet apart, as opposed to ninety feet in the big league. (See Figure 17.) The pitcher pitches from a rubber mat, the front of which is forty-six feet from the back point of home plate, as opposed to 60' 6" in the big league. The Little League fences are usually up to 200' from home plate, while big league fences average about 350'.

How children get onto teams varies from town to town. Call a club official if you need to know this information. Usually, under age nine or ten, the teams are put together by the club officials. They get the kids out at a "try-out" where each one is rated on a point scale. Then they try to give each team the same number of above and below average players. They do their best,

Figure 17 (cont.)
REGULATION LITTLE LEAGUE FIELD

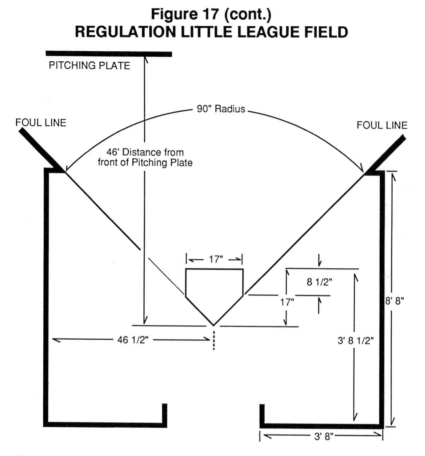

Diagram showing layout of batter's box and compulsory dimensions

and it usually helps, although you never know until the umpire says "play ball" what they will do.

Usually at about nine or ten the coaches get together and draft their team just like in the pros. They have the kids' last year ratings and their own notes. More experienced coaches, or guys like me who coach several sports, usually know the best talent. We draw lots to see who goes first and then go in rotation.

In Little League there is no rule requiring that every player get into the game. However, nearly all clubs have a local rule requiring at least one "at bat" and two defensive innings. Games last for six innings. Many clubs require the coach to bat every player at the game in rotation, particularly in younger age groups. Check with your local board and get a copy of the rules pertaining to your club. Some clubs follow Official Little League rules (which I prefer), others are independent and make up their own. If a coach violates this rule, talk to him or call the club president.

Players are allowed to steal a base under certain conditions. First of all, they are not allowed to take a lead. This is because the distance between bases is so short. They can leave the base when the pitched ball reaches the batter. Again, local rules sometimes prohibit stealing at all, or prohibit only stealing home.

A runner usually advances to the next base, or beyond, upon a hit ball which lands in fair territory. If it touches the foul line it is still fair. It must pass first or third base in fair territory to be fair. If it touches in fair territory and then rolls foul before it gets to first or third base, it is foul as soon as the fielder retrieves it. If it touches in fair territory and rolls foul after it passes third base (or first base if hit to that side) or any part of these bases, then it is fair. If a player touches the ball in fair territory and then it goes foul, it is a fair ball! Misunderstandings as to this rule are usually good for a groan or two from parents during a game.

A runner is "forced" and must advance to the next base if the bases behind him are filled and a hit ball touches fair ground. So if a runner is on first, she must get to second; if runners are on first and second, they both must advance, and so forth. If a runner however is on second, and no one is on first, then he is not "forced" and can stay on that base if it would be dangerous to try to advance (e.g., a ball hit towards third base).

However, if the ball is hit up in the air, the runner should not advance too far until the ball is caught or missed. If he does, and the ball is caught in the air, then he must get back to that base before the ball gets there or risk being "doubled-up," meaning that both he and the batter are out. After a fly ball is caught, then the runner may "tag-up," e.g., touch the base and advance. This often happens with a runner at third when a fly ball is caught deep in the outfield. The runner can usually tag third base and get home before the throw gets to the catcher.

There is a rule called the infield-fly rule, which prevents infielders from intentionally dropping a pop-up to get a double play. The rule is that if the ball can be caught by an infielder with ordinary effort, when there are runners on first and second or bases are loaded, with none or one out, the batter is automatically out and runners can tag up and advance at their own risk. If the ball is dropped the runner need not advance. Many Little League umpires do not use this rule. I think they just forget to call it or don't understand it.

Tie regulation games which are halted by the umpire, due to weather, curfew, or light, are resumed at the same point where they were stopped, so long as four innings have been completed. If one team is ahead at that time, or if the home team is ahead or tied after 3 1/2 innings, it is a regulation game. If a game has not reached four innings, or 3 1/2 innings with the home team losing, it is "no-game," and all scores are erased. The game is played over. This is another rule which should be understood by parents.

A batter must stand in the batter's box. The batter's box ends four inches away from the side of the plate, if the batter crosses that line, especially if he steps on or in front of the plate when he swings, he is out upon hitting the ball.

If a batted ball hits a runner, if he interferes with a fielder, or if he doesn't slide into a base when the fielder at the base has the ball, he is out.

If a child leaves the base too soon, before the pitch reaches the batter, he must go back. He is not automatically out. If the ball is hit the runner must go back to the base, or to the next unoccupied base.

When a batter hits a ball which lands in foul territory, it is a strike unless the batter already has two strikes. In that case it doesn't mean anything. There is no limit to the number of foul balls which may be hit. A foul pop-up may be caught in the air for an out. Runners in that case may tag up and advance.

Other information may be taken from the following glossary.

GLOSSARY: Let's Talk Baseball

Sometimes at a baseball game you think you are in a different country with the jargon. Here are some terms so you can "talk baseball" as well as anyone. Some things have been described in the body of the book, so there is no need to repeat them here.

APPEAL — When a runner leaves a base too soon, does not tag up on a fly ball, misses a base when running; or when a batter swings the bat breaking the wrist with a ball called, a fielder may claim this violation and request the umpire's judgment. If the ump saw it, he will make the appropriate call, e.g., out, strike, return to base, etc.

BACKSTOP — The fence which partially encloses the batter's box from behind. It usually is tall enough to keep foul tips from going too far back and hitting your car, although some do get past the fence and the cheers will indicate if a car gets hit. When you do batting practice it's good to have something tall behind the batter to stop the ball. It saves a lot of chasing time. I've used a piece of plywood or a large cardboard box if there is no backstop.

BALK — I've never seen this called in Little League play, but it's in the rule book. A balk is the penalty for the pitcher faking a pitch to get a base-runner off balance. I guess since there is no stealing until the ball reaches the batter, the main thing a balk is supposed to eliminate can't happen anyway. If the pitcher is on the rubber and makes any motion indicating the beginning of the pitch, or feints a throw to a base, the runners are all allowed to advance one base. It is also a balk if the pitcher does not come to a complete stop between his windup and the pitch. In 1988 umpires started calling this in the major leagues and it lead to a period of much confusion.

BALL — A pitch outside of the strike zone. Four balls in one at bat entitle the batter to go to first base, called a "walk." It kills me when I hear a kid get three balls, and then the coaches or parents start yelling to him — "a walk is as good as a hit," or "swing only if it's good." Sure, with a 3-0 count I agree, but other than that we should always encourage a child to hit. There are times when a walk is a good idea, but it galls me to see a kid up who is obviously struggling, and have people encourage him to look for a walk so he gets on base. It may be good for those who think winning is important, but the message to the kid is: "walk, because we don't have faith in your bat." If you don't have faith, he'll never find it!

BASE BAG — There are three of them: one at each corner of the infield. While on base the runner can't be tagged out, unless he was forced to advance. The fourth base is called "home plate."

BATTER'S BOX — This is a 3' by 6' box on either side of the plate, starting 27 1/2" behind the back tip of the plate, and coming up four inches from the side of the plate. The batters must be entirely inside the box while hitting the ball. Usually, Little League fields are not "lined," and there is only an imaginary batter's box. I like to tell kids to stand as far back in the batter's box as the ump will allow — use the whole 27 1/2" — it gives you a split second more to see the ball, and it seems to shrink the strike zone.

BREAKING BALL — A pitch which carries a lot of spin designed to make it curve or break direction as it travels towards the batter, making it necessary for the batter to adjust the swing accordingly. The ball breaks because the treads on the ball grab into the air and the ball is nudged in a new direction. I rarely hear of kids being taught to throw a curve, slider, knuckle ball, sinker, hook, or other breaking pitch. The word is that a kid can hurt his arm snapping his wrist if he does it wrong. The rules don't prohibit it, but I've seen umpires tell the kid to stop. I remember one kid who had a natural curve ball; he didn't know he was throwing one. I had to explain to the ump that it's not an illegal pitch, and besides the kid couldn't stop it.

BULLPEN — A separate section in foul territory where the pitchers sit, in the big league. It's near where they warm up in case they get called in. I'm not sure why it needs to be so separate, but pitchers are often pretty flaky, so leave 'em there.

CATCH — Okay, we probably all know what a catch is. But the rule is that you have to possess the ball long enough to prove complete control of the ball. If you catch it squarely, and then fall and dislodge the ball, it's not a catch. Different kinds of catches include a basket catch, over the shoulder, diving, and backhand. A catch is also called a stab and a grab. A ball that bounces just as a player catches it is called a trap. One that bounces just before a player catches it is a short-hop.

CHOKE-UP — Holding the hands further up the handle of the bat, a few inches closer to the fat end. It makes the bat lighter and easier to control. Smaller players or players with two strikes should always choke-up. Bat speed is important. It does however reduce power.

COUNT — The number of balls and strikes on a batter at any moment.

CRANE — When a pitcher lifts his foot high in the air when he is about to pitch. It looks like a crane lifting his leg.

DEAD BALL — A ball out of play because play is suspended such as a batter hit by a pitch, a runner hit by a batted ball, a ball which goes into the dugout or any other out of bounds area.

DIAMOND — A name given to the infield, outlined by the four basepaths and roughly resembling a diamond.

DOUBLE PLAY — When the defense gets two outs during one play. Usually when a runner is on first, and an infielder touches second and first base with the ball before both runners get there. These are force plays. Another double play often occurs when a fly ball is caught and the ball is thrown to a base before a runner can get back to tag up.

DUGOUT — The place where players sit while waiting to play. Usually in the big leagues it's an area with a bench, dug a few feet into the ground (it's cooler).

ERROR — The failure of a fielder to catch a ball which should have been caught with ordinary effort, or an errant throw resulting in prolonging the at bat or a runner's advance. Mistakes or slowness are not errors. An error is also called a boot, a muff, or throwing the ball away.

FOLLOW THROUGH — In hitting or pitching, allowing the bat or the pitcher's hand to continue along its normal course after the hit or pitch occurs. It allows for more control and power in both activities.

FORCE PLAY — When a runner must advance on a batted ball because all bases behind them are filled with runners. For instance, if bases are loaded, everyone must reach the next base. If there is a man on first and second both must advance to make room on first for the batter. A man on first only must get to second to make room for the batter. The forced runner is out if a fielder with the ball touches a base the runner must advance to before the runner gets there.

FORFEIT — A game which is won or lost by a call of the umpire for certain violations such as failure to place nine players in the field, delay of game, or a persistent rule violation.

FOUL — The foul territory is the area outside of the two foul lines, the first and third base lines, out to a fence area then straight up. A foul ball is a batted ball which lands in foul territory. Note: If it rolls back into fair territory before it passes a base, it is a fair ball. A foul tip is a ball nicked by the bat. If the catcher catches a foul tip on the third strike the batter is out.

FUNGO — An extra thick bat used for hitting grounders or fly balls for defensive practice. It makes it easier to hit the ball. Remember, I recommend just throwing the ball to your child for accuracy. It's tough to hit consistently for accuracy.

GAMER — A kid who really hustles and likes the game. Also a game winning hit.

GROUNDER — A ball that hits and travels or bounces along the ground in the infield.

GROUND RULE DOUBLE — A ball which bounces over the outfield fence, or is touched by a fan after bouncing in fair territory. The batter advances to second base.

HIT — When a batter safely advances at least to first base on a batted ball which lands in fair territory. Hits are singles, doubles, triples, or home runs. A home run with bases loaded (runners on each base) is a grand slam. A pop-up or fly ball is one hit up into the air. If it drops in between the outfield and infield it is a bloop or a Texas leaguer; it is said to drop into shallow outfield. Hitting the ball is also called sticking it, poking it, rapping it, or nailing it. A line drive hit is the most desirable hit, also called a rope.

INNING — The game is divided into nine innings. An inning is played when each team has had a chance to bat. Once each team has made three outs in its half-inning, a new inning starts. If the score is tied after nine innings, the game continues until an inning ends with one team ahead.

INTERFERENCE — Running into or obstructing a fielder trying to make a play, moving in a manner to hinder or distract a batter. In the first instance the runner is out and other runners return to the last base they touched. The ball is dead. In the latter the umpire warns the fielder to stop. If a fielder interferes with a runner, it is called obstruction.

LEAD — When a runner takes a few steps towards the next base before the ball is pitched. This is not allowed in Little

League play on the smaller fields for age twelve and under. You cannot leave the base until the ball has reached the batter.

PITCH — We already talked about breaking balls. A hard straight pitch is a fast ball. Another good pitch is a change of pace when the ball is thrown slowly after a normal wind-up. It confuses the batter who starts to swing too early, then suddenly has to slow down to wait for the ball. It is a pitch which is often said to "screw the batter into the ground." A ball thrown at a batter is a beanball or a dust-off pitch. At advanced levels, such pitching tactics are encouraged to get a batter worried or distracted. It's an unfortunate fact of life at that level. A pitch which can't be caught is a wild pitch; if it can be but isn't caught the catcher is charged with a passed ball. If the pitcher wets the ball, causing the ball to move erratically, it is illegal, called a spit ball. Another way to get a ball to move is to scuff up a part of it so the scuff catches air as the ball spins. Jim Niekro was suspended in 1987 for ten days for carrying an emery board in his pocket to scuff the ball. The knuckleball or screwball is a pitch which can break several times or in any direction. When a pitcher raises his hands above his head just before pitching, it is a wind-up, then he lifts his left foot (righty pitchers) into a crane position and drives himself towards the batter into a stretch, after releasing the ball his hand continues on a follow-through.

STRIKE ZONE — The area over home plate from the batter's knees to his armpits. If any part of a pitched ball passes through this area the batter will be charged with a strike. Three strikes are an out. Strike zones often vary by umpires, and this is the source of most arguments in baseball.

TAG — Touching a runner not on base with the ball, or with a glove containing the ball.

WARMUPS — Exercises done before any athletic endeavor to slowly warm up or heat and extend muscles. I'll include more on this in the last chapter.

4.

RUNNING AND SLIDING

One great thing about baseball is that the part which is the most fun — hitting — is also the easiest to teach. Running, however, is like fielding, if you don't have it naturally, as some kids do, you can improve it only with a great deal of practice. I repeat, the old adage that you can't make a kid a fielder, or pitcher, or runner is not true. But it does take longer, and the key is just doing a lot of it. By the same token, if kids don't get sufficient leg exercise they can get slower; I've seen it happen.

Usually kids who are slow play third base, first base, or catcher. It's because they don't need as much speed or range at those positions. They do need quickness and good reflexes; they just don't need speed.

At young ages, you can increase speed somewhat by running wind sprints. Tell your child to run a half dozen thirty yard dashes. It will give her additional leg strength to get up to speed more quickly. Acceleration is based on leg strength. Make sure she runs on the balls of her toes, head and shoulders forward, arms churning up and down. Running up stairs or hills is good for quickness. Again — there is a difference between quickness and speed. Quickness is mobility in a short distance. A child can improve quickness more easily than speed.

Defensive players, as noted earlier, always need to be on their toes, weight forward, body bent forward and down to lower the center of gravity. Also, keeping the weight on the toes allows the infielder to dance, spring, and hop as needed both to field the ball and quickly switch to a throwing stance.

RUNNING BASES

Base runners have to do the same thing. Weight down and forward, on the toes, ready to spring. When a player is running to a base, especially first base, it should always be as fast as possible. How many times have we seen a player out at first base because he turned to see where the ball was, or slowed down just before he got to the base? He should just put his head down and run like there's no tomorrow.

When a runner runs to first base on an infield hit, she runs hard and through the bag. There is no rule on which way to turn, and she can safely return to first as long as she did not attempt to go to second base. If the ball is hit to the outfield the runner should run a hook pattern. (See Figure 18.) This means that the runner makes an arc, about six to eight feet into foul territory on a Little League size field. Start to make the arc about halfway or more to first base.

When a runner is going to pass a base, he plants his left foot on the inside corner of the bag and leans into the turn. This can save a lot of time, a step or two. (See Figure 18.) The base can be touched with either foot, so don't get jumbled up, however, the left foot is preferable.

Once the runner gets to a base he has to look at the ball and decide whether to advance further. Runners should always know where the ball is, and watch or anticipate where and how hard it will be thrown. Your child should listen to the base coach, but rely on his own judgment too. I like my runners to pretend they are going to stop (if the outfielder is preparing to throw), but get as much ground as they can. Then, if the throw is not good, or if it's not to the base in front of them, they can advance to that base. A runner who hits the ball to the outfield should go about 1/4 - 1/3 of the way to second base, and then see if the throw is other than to the bag in front of him — if not, he goes. Many kids can make the remaining forty feet before someone can catch the

Figure 18
RUNNING A BASE

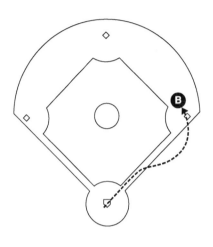

Hook pattern rounding first base

Plant foot on inside corner and lean in

throw and relay it to the second baseman. After some practice a child will know what he or she can do.

Remember, we talked a bit in Chapter 2 about throwing in front of the lead runner. Well, this also means that the lead runner should look for chances to advance an extra base, especially if the ball isn't thrown ahead of her. Runners should always make things happen, take a wide turn at a base, not so wide that you can't get back safely, but wide enough to draw a throw. If the throw is bad, you go. Some boys and girls are so fast that they automatically go when the ball is thrown behind them — because they know they will beat the relay.

STEALING BASES

Stealing bases is the worst part of Little League ball. The distance between bases is very short, and the inability to take a lead makes it very, very hard to steal except on a passed ball. However, there are so many passed balls and wild pitches that runners pretty much advance at will. Occasionally you get a decent catcher who will hold it down, but stealing on passed balls dominates the game. I don't like it, but that's the way it is.

So I keep my players running. When they are on third base, I tell them to nonchalantly move towards the catcher after the ball passes the batter, and if they advance ten feet, to steal as soon as the catcher throws back to the pitcher. If the pitcher is on the mound, the play will work. I can't say I like it. It's just not baseball to have so many runs based on steals. Some leagues prohibit stealing, or at least stealing home. I agree with that — make them hit the ball. But until they change the rules, I will keep them running.

When you talk about running to your child, talk about the need to lower the center of gravity, stay on the toes, look for chances to run, and run hard when you go — it will help. Make a list of the basics and yell them out every so often. It works, repetition works. (See Figure 19.)

SLIDING

Sliding is an important part of base running. Many outs or successful steals are based on how good the slide is. I know that very few coaches teach it. It may be that the ground is too hard, or the coach doesn't feel he has time. But there are basics to sliding, and it can be practiced.

I have practiced sliding by getting a large piece of cardboard, like a refrigerator box, and laying it on the ground. The kids take off their shoes and run and slide on the cardboard. Remove any staples! It works and they love it. It's fun!

Figure 19
RUNNING POSITION

Ready to run

Proper position. Center of gravity low. Eyes straight ahead. Arms churning

The technique to sliding is demonstrated in Figure 20. The right leg is tucked in under the left, and the slide is pretty much flat on the butt. A lot of people turn on the slide, but that hurts more and raises the body surface. The key to sliding is to keep every part of the body low to the ground. So the best slide is one where the player is virtually lying down on his back at the time of contact. The players should avoid breaking the fall with their hands; it's very easy to sprain the wrist. Besides, the backside gives enough cushion. Keep the hands up, off the ground, but not so high that they can be tagged.

The player should slide away from the ball. On a throw from the outfield, slide inside the base (second base). For a play at the plate, slide to the umpire side of home plate, away from the throw. This is called a hook slide.

Figure 20
SLIDING

Some gung-ho players slide head first, diving at the base. It does get you there a bit more quickly, but is very dangerous. I was playing softball in 1985 when a teammate named Roy dove into second base, hit the ground, turned his back to the fielder, got a knee in the back, and broke his back. I've seen sprained wrists and bloody noses. Needless to say, at twelve years old or below these kids don't need to dive. I don't teach it to them, I don't encourage it. If it happens I caution the boy against it. It's not worth it.

5.

BASEBALL POSITIONS

At young ages, kids should play various, if not all, positions. They certainly should practice at different positions. Early in the season I have every boy or girl on the team pitch during practice. During defensive drills they play every position. I do this because it's good for them, and because it helps me to see what their skills are and who is best for the more important positions up the middle — shortstop, second base, centerfield. The earlier chapters of this book have identified some basics for all positions, and you should try to spend some time on each area. Emphasize hitting, but work also on fielding, throwing, and running.

This chapter will address each individual position, and will help you get a better understanding of defensive concepts from the very specific perspective of the individual position. This will add to your overview of the game, and put you in a better position to advise your child as to what position she should play and what to do in a given situation.

CATCHER

No one can pick up a team like a catcher. They face the team so are in the best position to encourage fellow players, keep them on their toes. A catcher should be a leader, an aggressive kid. He can really inspire the team from his vantage point.

It takes a special kind of kid to hang in at this position. It's tough to get kids interested in it, and even tougher to find a good one. If you want to guarantee that your child plays a lot in each game, tell him to be a catcher. He'll play all he wants at that position.

Catchers are usually pretty tough-minded kids. They have to be able to take some pain. The ball often will strain the thumb in the catching hand. They get bruised by the ball, and run over by runners. It's dirty and hot underneath all of the equipment. They are constantly getting up and down on every pitch, and must be into the game more than anyone on the field. I love catchers!

As noted earlier, catching is good for a big kid (or any size frankly) who has no speed or can't really play well defensively. There is a defensive position for everybody, if your child can hit she must find a position she can play.

Catchers must get used to the crouch, on the toes of both feet. If she is a righty, the right foot is back a bit. Weight should be forward on the balls of the feet, heels lightly touching the ground. Putting one knee down on the ground is no good. It reduces mobility, agility, and it increases the risk of injury. The upper leg is parallel to the ground, waist bent forward. (See Figure 21.)

Little League catchers often get too far back behind the plate. This is because they are worried about getting hit with the bat. They don't realize that the batter is stepping forward, his body moving towards the pitcher, and there is really no way the bat will hit them. They must get close to the batters, because that's where the strike zone is. If they move back too far, then the pitcher has to throw higher to reach the glove. Also, the strike zone will shrink to the umpire's perspective if he is too far back from the batter.

The catcher has to let the ball come to the glove. If she reaches out for it, then there is a chance the bat will nick the glove. This doesn't happen often, but the batter gets a free trip to first base when it does. Pitches above the waist should be caught with the fingers up, low pitches with the fingers down. The glove hand is soft, receiving the ball and gently pulling it back to the chest. Don't stab at it.

Figure 21
CATCHING POSITION

The catcher's free hand should be behind her back or behind her leg. Some kids put it behind the glove, and that's dangerous. It can get hit by the bat or by a foul tip. Keeping it behind some part of the body, fist clenched, will protect it.

One of the most important things a catcher does is to control the pitcher's tempo and his emotions. He should constantly talk to the pitcher. Remind him to keep pitching "over the top" instead of relaxing into a sidearm motion, and to follow through when he starts getting tired. He should remind the pitcher to drive hard off the back foot. The catcher should keep reminding the pitcher of the catcher's glove — "hit the glove, here it is, pop the glove, baby." The catcher should pound the glove with his free hand, move the glove around a little bit, open and close it, anything to get the pitcher to focus on the glove. The catcher should sometimes yell out "nice pitch" on a strike, even before the umpire calls it. If the ball is a bit out of the strike zone a quick snatch pulling the glove back into the strike zone can buy a strike sometimes. The catcher should slow the pitcher's rate of pitching

Figure 22
BLOCKING LOW PITCHES

Low pitch over the plate   *Low pitch to one side*

if he starts to rush. Stand up, walk around, slow the pitcher down so he takes time to concentrate.

If the catcher sees someone out of position he should tell them or tell the coach.

The second most important thing a catcher does is stop the low pitch. A pitch in the dirt is tough to catch, so the priority is to block it. Tell your child to drop to her knees, drop the glove low, fingers down, and concentrate on blocking the ball. If it goes into the glove, fine. Otherwise it will at least be nearby. If the pitch is low and to one side, drop the closest knee in front of the ball and try to keep the body facing forward to assist if the ball comes up. (See Figure 22.)

If your child is a catcher, ask the coach if you can borrow the gear, or keep it at home for the season. This way you can practice low pitches. Put some extra padding on the exposed areas such as the thighs and arms. Throw low pitches from about half the distance to the mound.

Another very important thing a catcher does is throw out people who are stealing. Usually in Little League a kid will steal only on a passed ball or wild pitch. So a good practice drill is to get your boy in a crouch position and throw the ball behind him to the backstop. He then should turn, run to the ball, take off his mask as he runs and throw it to the side, pick the ball up, and turn, firing the ball to second base. Practice this a dozen or so times each practice. After a while he will know how much time he has taken to get to the ball, and whether he will have a play. If there is another person around, have them run from first to second so timing can be learned. If the runner is stealing third, the catcher must be sure he has a play before throwing the ball. A bad throw will cost a run. This play, above all, should be practiced. A lot of coaches practice the throw to second — but the throw to third is more important. When a runner steals home on a passed ball, the catcher really needs to move quickly. He runs to the ball and snatches it to the pitcher covering home plate. It must be all one motion, and if done quickly the runner can be tagged.

The last thing I want to say about catchers is they need to be able to get the man out at the plate. Usually the ball is thrown to them hurriedly, off line or in the dirt. Let them practice getting throws into the dirt, so they learn how to stop a bad throw. They should stand right in front of home plate, and if the ball is going to get to them, they turn and block the plate with their left foot, catch the ball with two hands (it must be two hands, a collision is coming), and bring the glove downward quickly to tag the feet. The runner must slide, or he is out, so the tag will always be low. The catcher should have his mask off, in fact the mask should come off automatically every time the ball is hit. It's a lot easier to catch a ball at the plate if you can see it, so get the mask off. (See Figure 23.)

Catchers should also practice catching foul tips (throw the ball straight up), and throwing to first base on bunts. Tell him to make sure he has an open angle to the first baseman so he doesn't hit the runner in the back. The key is to approach the ball from the left side and, if necessary, take a few steps towards the pitcher before throwing.

Figure 23
PLAY AT THE PLATE

Awaiting the throw. Left foot on the plate

Proper positions. In front of plate, left leg blocking plate, two hands on the ball, face mask off, bring the right knee and glove down quickly and tag low

FIRST BASE

I played a lot at first base over the years. I was tall (I'm 6'4"), decent glove, slow, and I could hit. These are good ingredients for a first baseman. Add in a lefty, and it's perfect. (A lefty doesn't have to turn around and catch the ball backward like a righty does.)

In Little League play, first base is very important. You're whole infield is as good as your first baseman. The shortstop can make a great play, a good throw, and if the first baseman drops it, or comes off the bag too early, the fielding effort was worthless. If your child can catch hard line drives, he or she can play at first.

Figure 24
FIRST BASEMAN'S STRETCH

See path of ball before stretching   *Then stretch*

A first baseman has one main job. He has to catch the ball when thrown to him. As soon as a grounder is hit to another fielder, the first baseman must get to the bag as quickly as he can. He doesn't have to watch the ball, he has to look at the bag and get to it quickly. This is because we want him to be ready for the throw and to present a good target for the throw. When he gets to the bag he puts his back foot's toe, the foot opposite his glove hand, on the side of the bag and faces the fielder with the glove chest high. He doesn't stretch yet, not until he sees where the ball is going to go. Then he steps towards the ball, stretching as far as he needs to catch the ball for the out. (See Figure 24.)

If the throw is bad, the job is to stop it. If she can do that while touching the bag, swell, but if she has to leave the bag to catch the ball she must do so. Otherwise, the batter will go to second base and be in scoring position.

The toughest ball for a first baseman to catch, as with the catcher, is one in the dirt. Even if she is a good fielder, she is handicapped by the fact that her foot must stay on the bag, limiting her agility and reflexes. I used to practice catching balls thrown in the dirt with full catcher's gear on and a "cup." This eliminated my fear of the bad hop into the face, chest, or neck. I learned to keep my head down, eyes on the ball. I was able to develop concentration, and a sense for what the ball would do. First basemen have the biggest glove in the field, and that helps. I've seen first basemen who can stretch into a full split; that really looks sharp if you can do it.

If the throw is wide to the left, the first baseman's first thought should be to catch the ball, and tag the runner.

In Little League, a lot of throws are high. The first baseman should practice the timing needed to jump for the ball. If it's clearly out of reach, she should not waste time looking at it, but turn and run to where it will go — she may be able to stop the runner from advancing to second. She should make sure she doesn't collide with the runner when she does — the guy will be going full speed, and that can hurt.

When a grounder is hit to the first baseman, or between her and the second baseman, she must always try to get it. I've seen a lot of grounders go between the two fielders because the first baseman hesitates, feeling he had to cover the bag. On a grounder like that, the pitcher has to cover first base. You always, always try to make the field play. It's good to practice the lob from the first baseman to the pitcher. It's a tough play for the pitcher, since he is on the run and must look for the ball, then find the bag. The idea is to get the ball to the pitcher as soon as possible. Visibly hold it in the hand so the pitcher can see it and lob it to his glove. (See Figure 25.)

The first baseman also has to be ready to catch foul pops to the left side. The dugouts and fences are pretty close, so she needs to practice to know where they are.

A nervewracking play for the first baseman occurs when a runner is on third. I remember a play I was involved in when the shortstop got a grounder, looked at the runner on third to hold him there, and then threw to me. It was the tying run in the game, and just as the shortstop started to throw to me the runner on third broke for home, and he was fast. Out of the corner of my eye I saw him running, and I sensed that he might beat my

Figure 25
LOB TO THE PITCHER

Proper lob. Show the ball and lob before pitcher reaches base

throw home, so I came off the bag, went to the ball, caught it, and threw home. It was a smart play, my coach told me. The runner would surely have beaten the throw otherwise, it was just too bad that I threw the ball over the backstop.

Once the batter goes to second base, then the first baseman is free to do whatever he thinks is needed. If the pitcher goes to back up third base, the first baseman can run in to be the cut-off at the plate. Otherwise he can go and back up the catcher. If the ball will be thrown to second base, he must stay and back up that throw. That's about it. Life at first base is really pretty simple.

SECOND BASE

In Little League, particularly under age eleven, the second baseman is going to get the most grounders, not the shortstop. The shortstop does not even get the second most, the pitcher gets the second most grounders. The shortstop gets the third most plays, and the first baseman is right there with him.

The younger kids get the bat around slowly, and drop the right side. So most balls go to the right side, right at the second baseman. Kids have a tendency to play too close to the bag at second, but the proper positioning is about 1/3 of the way to first base and eight feet outside of the baseline.

A second baseman has to be able to stop grounders. He doesn't need a good arm, guys with good arms go to shortstop or third, but he does need to be quick. He's got to run the grounders down, at least knock them down, so he can throw to first. He needs to be smart, too. There is a lot of action, and we want somebody who can think.

When I think of second basemen, I think of smaller players. Good glove, quick, don't need a good arm. Remember, in baseball anybody of any size, speed, or strength can play — if he is willing to practice and develop some simple skills. I had a kid two years ago named Danny, one of the smallest kids in the league. He couldn't throw hard, and couldn't hit the ball out of the infield, but he was tough, and he wanted to play ball. He played with his friends every day. He played second base and did a good job. He was so tough minded that I even had him play catcher a few times in a pinch.

Chapter 2 discussed infielding generally, the need to stay low, weight forward, bend the knees, keep your head down on the ball, get the glove on the ground and raise it forward to the ball in a scooping motion. An infielder has to be able to dance, up on the toes. He springs to the ball, and hops into his throwing stance. If you look at the pros, they are always dancing around out there. And you've got to want the ball, hope it gets hit to you, and think about where you will throw it, before the ball is ever pitched. Talk to your son about these things, read the key points of this book to him, a little at a time, and then repeat the key phrases in this paragraph to him while you hit or throw, preferably throw grounders to him.

Second basemen must know what to do with the ball when they get it. If there is nobody on, they go to first. Man on first, they throw to the shortstop for the force at second. If she is close to the bag, take a step and lob the ball to the shortstop. If she is further away, pivot on the toes and throw sidearm.

Man on first and the ball is hit to the left side, the second baseman goes to second base and waits on the outside of the base to catch the throw from the shortstop or third baseman, and then steps on second and sees if he can get the ball to first for a double play. It happens rarely in Little League so the second baseman needs to know how close the batter is to first. There are a number of ways to pivot on second base, depending on timing and the situation. You can practice these by changing the timing and speed of your throw. If he's too close for a play, hold onto the ball — you don't want to throw it away. If there's a man on first and second, same thing, look for the force at second. Get the sure out. There are times you want to go to third I suppose, but in Little League play, go for the out. (See Figure 26.)

With bases loaded and less than two outs, the coach has a choice. In a close game, I always say throw home if you think you can stop the run — that's baseball, that's defense. Some coaches will not have faith in the catcher, or the second baseman's arm, and will say get the sure out — go to second base with it. Tell your son to ask the coach. My attitude is to teach them right, but different people will have different views about what's right.

If there's a man on third, and he is not forced to run home, then the infielder gives him a look before throwing for the force at second or first. If the runner is going, then throw home and get him out. Again, the purpose of defense is to stop runs. I say that's the way the game should be taught.

The second baseman is also the primary receiver of pop-ups for his side of the field, covering the space between the pitcher and first baseman. Anything behind the pitcher or significantly behind the first baseman, he should get to the ball and call for it. The toughest catches are "Texas-leaguers," shallow pops to the outfield. He has to turn and run, timing a leap for the ball. Practice these.

The second baseman is the cut-off for outfield singles if the ball is hit to his side of the outfield and no one is on base. Read Chapter 2 for the cut-offs when men are on base. Almost any time there are men on base, first or second, the second baseman's responsibility on a single is to cover second base. Other

Figure 26
SECOND BASE

Lob to shortstop if close

Sidearm if ball hit in the hole

Practice the pivot throw for double play

Tagging: straddle base and tag low

players will cut off throws to third or home. Now, if the ball is hit deep, past the outfielder to the fence, then the second baseman must go out to assist the relay. He is not really a cut-off, technically, at that point, he is just going out to make a relay.

On steals, I usually have the second baseman back up the shortstop on the throw from the catcher. This could be argued, I know, but that's how I do it. In the big leagues, it depends on whether the batter is righty or lefty, and where the ball might be hit. Usually on a righty batter the second baseman will cover for the steal, because the ball will more likely be hit to the shortstop, and you want him to stay put while the runner at first is breaking for second. Well, in Little League the kid can't steal till the ball gets to the batter, so we don't have the same situation. I think the shortstop can see the play better from his position, he can see the runner, and I let him make the tag. The second baseman backs him up.

Finally, the second baseman covers first base on bunts to the right side. The first baseman goes for the bunt, and someone needs to cover first base. The shortstop will cover second base.

SHORTSTOP

I'm not going to repeat every thing I said in Chapter 2 and summarized for the preceding section on second basemen. A lot of the new material relevant to second basemen also pertains to shortstops.

By the time kids are playing "major league" baseball (in Little League, eleven and twelve year olds play in the "major league," it is the high point of Little League, before the kids move to the larger fields), the shortstop becomes the cornerstone of the defense. She has to have a good glove, because the batters start to get around on the ball and more balls get hit to that position. She also has to have a good arm, because it's the longest infield throw, even longer than the third baseman (if they are playing the right positions), and she has to hurry the throw to beat the runner. A shortstop put-out is a pretty thing to see at Little League level. Many times the throw is late or high. Shortstop is another position for natural leaders.

A shortstop is usually the natural athlete who is born ready to play. He can do it all, and at that position you need it all. Most teams put their best all-around player at shortstop (when he is not pitching). This doesn't mean your son or daughter can't play shortstop, it just means he or she has to be the best if they want to play shortstop. And as I noted earlier, you don't have to be born with it, plenty of kids who are just average athletes work daily on their skills, and they become good enough to do the job. Yes, your child can learn to do anything in baseball, even pitch, if you practice long and hard enough. My son Joey is a really good hitter, so was Jackie, but Joey wants to pitch. He throws hard enough, but needs control. I didn't have him pitching for the first few years, but he has been practicing. He wants to pitch and by gum, I think he's going to make it some year.

Back to shortstops, since they should usually play as deep "in the hole" as possible (that's back, towards the outfield), they face a long throw. So more than any other infielder, they have to make the transition from fielding to throwing as quickly as possible. This transition involves two moves. The first is to get the ball out of the glove into the throwing hand, and the second is to hop into a set throwing position. See Chapter 2 on throwing positions. So when you practice with your son for shortstop, focus on making the transition quickly — talk about the need for quickness, practice it over and over.

With a man on first, I like the shortstop to try to make the double play himself. If he is too far from second base, then he obviously must throw the ball, but on a shot to the left of the shortstop he should think about doing it himself. The throw to the second baseman always runs the risk of being a problem. The second baseman takes time to change directions, and his throw is often off balance. If the shortstop does it himself, all of these risks are eliminated. I know that this is not the case on the big league fields, but there are a number of things different for the smaller fields, and this is one of them. Big league shortstops are too far from the bag to make double plays by themselves, it's as simple as that. It's the same way with the cut-off situation on a single with no one on base. I like the outfielder to throw directly to the base, that is, the so called cut-off man stands on second base, and the other guy backs him up. This is because the throw is so short, the outfielder can reach easily. I've always seen coaches send out a cut-off man on a throw towards second, and the cut-off man is ten feet from the outfielder. It doesn't make sense to do a cut-off just to do a cut-off, the game always has to make sense, and in Little League you have to adjust a bit, particularly for eleven and twelve year olds.

The shortstop has all shallow pop-ups on his side of the diamond and behind the third baseman. He is playing deeper than the third baseman, and he can cover behind him more easily. Obviously, you always have to call for the ball.

As far as calling for the ball goes, I am a bit of a renegade here. Many coaches teach that the first guy who calls for a ball gets it. I teach that the second guy, or last guy, who calls for the ball gets it, but he has to call off the first player very loudly and repeatedly. I do this for several reasons. First, the first guy who calls often does so too soon, out of instinct; second, the wind can change circumstances very quickly; third, the second guy who calls had more time to make a judgment that his position is better. Not that he is a better catcher, but that he is in a better position, and what he is doing is calling the first guy off. In any event, if two guys call for the ball, someone has to get it, and the rule should be a firm one either way. They are some general rules of priority the coach may set, although I've rarely seen coaches do this at the Little League level. For instance, the centerfielder has priority over anybody, an outfielder has priority over an infielder, a shortstop and second baseman have priority over their side of the infield as against other infielders, the catcher has priority over no one (because of the glove not being made for pop-ups). Obviously, players should not be too quick to call for the ball, and make sure they know it will land in their territory.

As with what I said about second basemen, if there is an unforced player on second or third, the shortstop should see if the runner is going, and fake a throw to get him to hold before throwing to first. The shortstop fake on this play, again, has to be the quickest of all, because he barely has time to get the ball to first as it is. Sometimes, all he will have time to do is give the runner a sharp look. This is a good move to practice a few times, have him fake a throw to third and then throw to first. Remember, he has to work on quickness or he will lose the guy at first.

The shortstop is the cutoff for singles to the left side with no one on, although I usually tell him to just stand on second, the second baseman backing him up. With a man on first, the throw going to third to stop the lead runner, the shortstop is the cut-off for all three outfielders. He must line himself up between the ball and third base, about fifteen to twenty feet from the bag. He has to know where the runner is, and if the batter is going to second base, he has to decide to cut the ball off and throw to second, or let the ball go through for a play at third. Obviously, if the throw is off-line, there will be no play at third anyway, and he must cut the ball off. On any ball hit past the outfielder on his side, the shortstop must go out far enough to get the relay throw, and he should know what he's going to do with the ball when he gets it — this is where the other infielders can help by telling him where to go. They should be looking at the runners to figure it out.

THIRD BASE

Usually, the fewest number of balls are hit to third base in Little League. In the pros it's called the "hot corner," but not in Little League. That's because the batters don't get a lot of bat speed, and tend to hit more to the right side. This is fine with me because it gives me a chance to use third base to try out different kids at infielding. It's also a place to put a kid who may be a bit weak defensively, but whose bat is too good to leave out of the lineup. Third base is also good for a kid who may have a decent glove, good reflexes, but is too slow to play shortstop or second. The two things a third baseman has to have are 1) a good arm to reach first base on grounders, and 2) be able to catch a throw from the catcher on guys stealing third. The second is the most important. If she misses the throw, the runner goes home, if the local rules allow it. This must be practiced. Straddle the back of the bag, and bring the ball down very quickly to a spot six inches in front of the bag and make the tag.

One way to practice this play is to tell your player she doesn't have to stand on the bag. A lot of times kids think they have to have a foot on the bag, and this reduces their mobility. They should stand straddling the back of the bag, facing the catcher. They must know that catching the ball, wherever it is, is more important than tagging the runner. Once she catches the ball, the next move is to bring the glove down quickly to the side of the base for the tag. The runner must slide!

As with the first baseman, the third baseman should know where the sideline fence is, for purposes of chasing down foul pop-ups. She should practice it. You can throw some pop-ups close to the fence. Tell her to see where the ball is going, head in that direction, take a quick glance at where the fence or dugout is, adjust accordingly, and then look again at the ball. It feels very awkward at first to take your eye off the ball, but it's not so bad after practicing it a few times.

I tell the third baseman to play in close. Usually the ball is not hit hard to third in Little League, grounders are often slow. The kids don't have the bat speed yet. I'd back her up for stronger hitters, but other than that I want her on the fringe of the grass. She has to learn to charge the slow dribbler. If it's slow enough it can be picked up with one hand, but this is done only if needed to beat the runner to first.

The third baseman is never a cut-off. She is in the pros for plays at the plate, but not in Little League. Coaches must be practical. She guards an important bag, and I want her there. She doesn't go out for relays, the shortstop does that. On plays to home plate the pitcher is my cut-off in Little League. If the pitcher is backing up third, then the first baseman comes in if she is free. Third basemen guard third base, that's it!

OUTFIELD

In youth baseball, left field is a very lonely position. I said it several times in connection with other positions, but the players, until they are about twelve, don't get the bat around quickly enough, the pitchers are too fast. The ball is usually hit to right or right centerfield. With my fast pitchers, I always put my best outfielder in right field. If I have a kid pitching who is slow, then I'll put my strength in centerfield. The right fielder, in any event, needs to be a decent catcher, and has to have the strongest arm in the outfield in order to get the ball to third base. More on that later. Left field is a place to learn. There is not a lot of action, not a lot of pressure.

Chapter 2 addressed some general defensive hints and practice drills for outfielders. The key ideas were to practice with soft balls, like tennis balls or rubber balls. Cork filled balls are also good for this. The child should catch the ball above eye level, palm facing outward. The main idea is to get quickly to the ball, and get under it — set to catch, and set to make the transition to throw the ball. Also, on a ball over the head, turn and run, don't back up. We also talked about throwing ahead of the lead runner, and hitting the cut-off. A brief summary is, for a single, that is a ball hit in front of the outfielder.

1) No one on. Get the ball to second base. Hit the cut-off, the shortstop or second baseman depending on what side of the field you are on. They should be standing on the base if the throw will be relatively short, or in front of the base about ten to fifteen feet for longer throws.

2) Man on first. Throw the ball towards third base. Make sure you hit the cut-off; it should be the shortstop.

3) Man on first and second. Throw home towards the pitcher. The pitcher will cut the ball off if the man on second stops at third.

4) Man on second. Same as #3. Except now the batter will look to go to second, so the cut-off has to work well.

5) Man on third. Same as #1. There's nobody on as far as the outfield is concerned. The man on third will score by the time the outfielder has the ball.

6) Bases loaded. Same as #3. The man on third will score, it's the man on second we want to stop; he is the lead runner for outfield purposes.

Also, if the ball is hit over your head to the fence, go get it as fast as you can. It will be a long throw, so shortstop or second base has to come out to help you. Don't look around! If you are too far away to throw anybody out, get the ball to the relay and let him "shoot" somebody.

Chapter 2 didn't cover fielding outfield grounders. These are among the toughest fielding plays to make in baseball. The fields the kids play on are often not rolled in the springtime, the grass may be kept at varying lengths, there are often ruts, holes, rocks,

Figure 27
FIELDING OUTFIELD GROUNDERS

or grass clumps. The ball can take wicked bounces. The fielder shouldn't charge the ball. Let it take a good bounce, and then lower one knee towards the ground. I like the knee barely touching the ground, so he can come up quickly if it bounces wide. There is no substitute for lowering the knee, the transition is not as important as it is in infield, so make sure you stop the ball, get the body in front of it. (See Figure 27.)

On steals, the centerfielder backs up second base, and the left fielder backs up third base. The left fielder may not get many hits in his direction, but there will be a lot of throws to third, and many will get through. The left fielder should hold his position until the ball passes the batters, and then get ready to break towards third base. If the runner goes, he keeps going. He heads obliquely to the foul line, so you get there before the ball does. Watch the throw — if it's wild, head where it is heading. Don't get too close to the third baseman, no closer than thirty feet. This is so the ball doesn't get past you. (See Figure 28.)

Figure 28
BACKING UP THIRD BASE

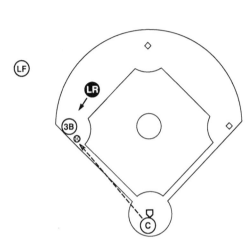

Left fielder heads to point about 20 feet behind third baseman

Finally, remember that runners will be tagging up on fly balls that the outfielders catch. So don't stand there gleaming over a great catch, get the ball to the base in front of the lead runner. It is very hard to get a guy at the plate, but third base for left fielders and centerfielders, and second base for the right fielder are good bets.

PITCHER

Last but certainly not least. Pitching is about the same at any level of baseball. Whether it's nine year olds or in the big leagues, a good pitcher is simply more valuable than anything else. This is just a fact of life. Championships are won at every level with good pitching. Look at the current New York Mets, they keep winning with pitching.

This truth doesn't diminish by one iota my statement that hitting is the essence of baseball. It's the fun of it, no doubt.

Hitting is for everybody, because everybody is a hitter. Pitching, however, is one of those things pretty much reserved for the gifted athletes. Some kids just have a knack for getting the ball over the plate. They have a gift for throwing hard. They can take pressure. These kids become pitchers, the "chosen people" of baseball. A pitcher is someone who can throw hard; the fastball is the cornerstone of pitching. Control comes second, and is essential if the boy doesn't throw very hard.

As with anything else, this doesn't mean your son or daughter is not a pitcher just because they can't hit the side of a barn from inside the barn. I said earlier that my youngest son had little control over his throws until he was eleven and, after four years of organized Little League ball, he finally got some pitching innings in 1988. He wanted to pitch, and he practiced at it. It paid off, and I gave him a shot. Coaches will respond to desire. Joey may never be a top pitcher, but he earned some innings, and that should tell you something. If you want to evaluate your child's pitching ability just have him or her pitch to you and see how many strikes they throw and whether they throw hard. Most pitches should be pretty close.

Arm Burnout

You will know pretty quickly if your child is a potential pitcher. However, this is one pointer where I caution against too much practice. The shoulder and elbow muscles and tendons are placed under a lot of stress when throwing a ball, and it is simply scandalous how many kids burn out their arms in Little League level play. They not only pitch at games and at practice, but because good pitchers are so rare, they are called on by their friends to pitch in sandlot games. In the big leagues they get four days rest, yet kids often pitch nearly every day. Don't let it happen. Set rules and enforce them. During the season, ensure that his or her arm gets rested. Above all, don't get out and practice pitching every day. I'd let Joey throw me a dozen or so pitches a few times a week, no more. The same holds true for any throwing at practice, you don't want too many hard throws a day, and you never throw hard until you have first had a few dozen soft throws to warm up.

Pitching Style

Okay, assuming you have a budding pitcher, what do you need to know about style? I'll discuss here the elements of a pitch, but the thing you start talking about right away is consistency. We want a robot on the mound, pitching pretty much with the same movement every pitch. Your child must understand this early on. (See Figure 29.)

1) Address the Batter. The pitchers in Little League usually have a small mound with a "rubber" on it. Tell your child to step on the rubber with the right foot, toes hanging forward beyond the rubber, and face the batter. Don't look at the batter, look only at the catcher's mitt. Hands are at the side. The left foot is slightly behind the right foot, to the left of the rubber. The pitcher should stand in the exact same spot on the rubber each time. If there is no rubber, have him or her draw one on the dirt, or make some mark. They must start thinking about consistency.

Figure 29
SIX PARTS OF THE PITCH

Address the batter   *The wind up*

Figure 29 (cont.)
SIX PARTS OF THE PITCH

The crane

The kick

The delivery

The follow-through

2) The Wind-Up. The wind-up is essentially a stretching motion, raising both hands up, usually over the head and coming together as they are lowered, coming to a complete stop. The pitcher starts a rocking motion forward and then back as he raises his hands.

3) The Crane. After the pitcher rocks back, he turns or pivots his right foot astride (still touching) the rubber and lifts his left leg, for balance, as he drops his hands and reaches back with his right (pitching) hand towards second base, extending his right arm straight back and downward. Lifting the left leg resembles a crane (bird) standing on one leg.

4) The Delivery. Kick, stretch and drive. At this point the pitcher rocks forward again, lunging his body, whipping open his left shoulder and leg, driving towards the batter. He drives hard with the back leg, for power, kicks out the front leg and, extending the arm, delivers the ball.

Pitching Tips

Now for some pitching tips, here are some more things to look for:

1) We mentioned consistency. We want the pitching style to look the same each time. Talk about this concept. It is not a combination of different moves, but is one continuous, smooth, but explosive action. Talk about gracefulness and smoothness. Also talk about power.

2) Reaching the arm down and straight back just before the delivery is done to promote full extension early in the pitch, and to prevent erratic movement at that critical moment. If the arm drifts off to first or third base slightly this can throw it off. One pro pitcher told me he liked to reach towards his back pocket with the ball, just to start at the same point each time.

3) Most pros lift their knee in the Crane position at least waist, and sometimes chest, high. It adds power by forcing the body to rock back further, but it can take some time for a youngster to adjust to the control needed. Some boys get into the habit of merely sweeping their left foot back towards second base, rather than lifting it, and that's a bad habit which must be corrected at once.

Figure 30
PITCHING GRIP

4) The delivery should be over the top, arm and ball as high as possible. Avoid sidearm throws. Kids sometimes go to sidearm when they are tired, or because they feel it gives more control. Sure, we've all seen good sidearm pitchers. Bret Saberhagen was one of the best relievers in the game in the early 1980s, and he threw sidearm/underhanded. But encourage your son or daughter to come over the top, or at least at a 3/4 (270 degree) angle. It's a more powerful pitch and is better for longevity of the arm, since it's not as herky-jerky as the sidearm throw.

5) The grip was covered in Chapter 2. Two fingers on the top touching threads. Thumb on left, and two pinky fingers on right, cradling the ball. The two top fingers should be fairly close together. The pitcher holds the ball with the fingers; it does not touch the palm and there should be a space in the thumb pocket. (See Figure 30.)

6) We talked about driving with the back foot, pushing off the end of the rubber. A lot of power can be added from the back foot. The pitcher should be told to try and draw from this driving power and relay the power into the pitch. It's a matter of perception.

Figure 31

Proper opening up

Insufficient opening up; left leg obstructs body

7) The left foot kicks out towards home and should land on the left side of a imaginary line from the back foot to the middle of the plate. This is called "opening up the door." The left foot, left shoulder, and left arm can be perceived as a door, opening up to the pitch. Often boys don't open up enough, stepping on instead of past the imaginary line, and the left foot then interferes with the follow through. I teach my pitchers to first perceive they are driving their left shoulder at the batter, and then open it up and swing the door. Avoid opening up too soon, losing power and control. The left foot should point to the plate when it lands, and not come down at an angle to the plate. Also, respecting the left foot, it should come down hard, pulling the pitcher into a complete follow through. Al Santorini, who was probably the best high school pitcher New Jersey ever had, and he pitched for a good number of years in the pros (now he has sons and is a Little League coach) told me that very few coaches realize the importance of landing hard with the stretch foot. Finally, the stretch

should be fairly long. A long stretch brings the center of gravity of the body down, and consequently the pitch comes down too. Low and outside pitches are the best pitches. (See Figure 31.)

8) We've mentioned the follow-through a few times. You should talk about it. However, a follow-through is a result of a good drive and stretch, and should happen automatically as a result of forward momentum. If a player has to try to follow-through, he just doesn't have enough forward momentum.

Pitching Strategy

At the younger ages the strategy is simple. Just get the ball over the plate. The pitcher who gives up the most walks will lose. At the older youth ages, we can begin to discuss some strategy.

1) Take your time. Too often the kids rush from one pitch to the next. They need to develop a rhythm, and they need to focus on concentration.

2) Hit the glove. The catcher's glove is the whole world to the pitcher. He should blank everything else out. Just think about the glove and try to hit it. As control comes, think about corners of the glove.

3) Get in front of the batter. The first strike is important. If you get two strikes, and no or one ball, then rear back and fire some heat! Don't let a batter beat you when you are ahead. You can afford to give up some control in favor of heat when you are ahead in the count.

4) Know the batters. If a batter won't swing, throw easy strikes. Fire heat at the good hitters.

5) If a ball is hit to the pitcher's left side, the pitcher must always break to cover first base. If he is not needed, he can stop.

6) If the lead runner is on first base, the pitcher backs up third. If the lead runner is on second, he is the cut-off at the plate. On a passed ball or wild pitch with a lead runner on third, he covers the plate.

7) Since the pitcher has the best view of the action on a hit ball, he or she should take charge on assisting fielders with where to throw the ball.

8) In Little League, pitchers can pitch only six innings a week, Sunday to Saturday; they must have at least one day of rest

Figure 32
SINKING FASTBALL

between appearances, and must rest three full days if they pitch over three innings in a game.

Types of Pitches

As noted earlier, a fastball is the bread and butter of pitching. At young ages it is pretty much the only pitch used. It's just a hard straight pitch. If the ball is gripped across the seams as in Figure 30, it will go straight, and even rise a bit as your child gets stronger. The great pitchers throw rising fastballs, and they are extremely difficult to hit with a bat moving in a downward arc. If your boy wants some variety, tell him to hold the ball along and on top of the two seams where they come together. (See Figure 32.) This will result in the ball's sinking a bit.

The curve ball is the second most popular pitch. It is much slower than a fast ball and, in the pros, a batter will often be off balance, swinging a bit too soon at a ball which is not only slow, it is curving right at him. Kids rarely throw curves before high school. Coaches don't know how to teach it, and that's good because it's tougher on the arm than a fast ball if it is thrown wrong. The main idea is to throw more with the middle finger and to snap the wrist sharply, giving the ball a sideways spin. As the wrist snaps it turns in towards the body. You and your child can try it, but don't concentrate on it. There are other pitches too, slider, split-finger fastballs, knuckleballs, change-ups. Let your child learn these in high school. He'll kill his arm trying to learn them too early. Besides, some local rules forbid "funny" pitches.

6.

ODDS AND ENDS

THE BEST AGE TO LEARN THE GAME

Aren't they too young to learn all this? What is a good age?

If your son or daughter is very young, under nine, then it will be a few years before a lot of this material will be used. The basics, especially the stuff on hitting and fielding should be started right away, to avoid bad habits. I pitched to my kids as soon as they could hold a bat. Remember Keith, a potential all star who lost two years because of dropping his right side. However, a lot of the refinements, the cut-off concept, covering positions, these things take time and maturity. I had a group of ten year old all-stars one year, and I started to give them more advanced cut-off concepts. I knew they would use little of it for a long time, but I had to start somewhere. Maybe if parents set the stage in the early years, it can happen by age ten. But if you can't, don't worry about it, concentrate on the basics, and save the advanced stuff for later on.

Believe me when I say there is no magic age. Look at the age of kids mastering moves in gymnastics, soccer, and other sports at seven and eight years old. It's not that the young kids can't learn. They just need someone who understands to teach them the concepts, and to drill them on them. There isn't anything in this book that's over their heads, just start somewhere, and the kids will absorb as much as you have the time and patience to teach them. Some things will take a few sessions, some more, but it will happen. Like learning how to whistle, suddenly one day it's there.

WINNING, WINNING, WINNING

Well, winning is like religion and politics. Everybody thinks they are right, and believes fiercely in their view. Some coaches think winning isn't just number one, it's everything. You always hear people say that if you are going to keep score, then you have to teach the kids to win, that if you tell a bunch of kids that winning is not important, they will all nod their heads and lower their eyes like angels, but underneath they are not really buying it. They have heard too much about winning, they know that most people consider it the most important thing. Well, I don't agree. Kids talk about winning, but they care more about how they feel about themselves. You start there.

I remember one year I was playing, I was in a terrible slump, the team was winning, but was that satisfactory to me? No way — I was playing lousy. Another year we lost a championship game, but I hit a home run. How did I feel? You guessed it. Sure I wanted to win, but the homer is all I remember, not the score.

All right, maybe winning is important in the pros, of course it is. And maybe even in high school, where scholarship money never looks at anybody on a team with a 3-26 record. But in Little League, it's just not important. Parents think it's important, but the kids forget the game and the score as soon as they hit the nearest pool.

I tell my kids something they can believe, I tell them everything I just said above, and I tell them that winning is never important in Little League, but it is always fun to win. That's the truth. They can relate to that. Don't put pressure on them to win. It's not important; their feelings are what's important.

HOW CAN I GET MY KID INTERESTED IN BASEBALL?

The most important way is by avoiding the negative stuff, as we have repeated many times in this book. If your child is afraid of the ball, fearful of being embarrassed, or tired of your impatience (if you are yelling at him, and getting annoyed or frustrated), he will never be interested. Tell her she is a hitter already, and you are going to work with her to develop it. Communicate, discuss the things in this book — talk baseball, go to a pro game or to a local high school game. Watch some baseball on TV, work with your child in trying to collect a whole series of baseball cards. If you go out and coach her and she gets better, you won't have to worry about interest.

One afternoon last week I got home from work and Joey was on the stoop with a ball and two gloves waiting for me. "Hey Dad, want to catch a few?" Interest? I can't turn it off. He tells his friends that I'm his buddy, and baseball is one of the main reasons for our friendship. You work closely with your child on something like this, and he will not only be interested in baseball, he'll become interested in you, and you in him or her. How can you lose?

BEHAVIOR AT GAMES

I'm not going to tell you to just sit there and be quiet. I'm not going to tell you to reduce your energy by one iota. But if you read this book carefully, you know what to do at games. First of all, we don't want to add any pressure to our children, or anyone's children. Second, we want to say intelligent, helpful things like "keep your eye on the ball," "keep the elbow up," "on your toes," "two outs," "you're a hitter," — things that will help her to remember the basics. If she swings and misses, yell "good cut." I hate it when a kid swings at a bad pitch, and the coach yells "bad pitch." For goodness sakes, he already knows that, tell him to get a better pitch next time. Be positive. If he strikes out swinging, I always clap my hands. If they are swinging, I know they are going to hit it at some point. So if they strike out swinging, I want them to be happy. If they take a called third strike, and the ball was over the plate I don't yell anything. I take them to the side and we talk about the fact that they can't have fun unless they swing the bat.

Another thing you can do at games is get to know the other parents on your team. It's really a beautiful thing when teams become one big family. Most of mine have been that way, because I promote it as a high priority. It makes everything more loose, more relaxed, and that's better for the kids. It also can lead to some rewarding friendships and to a deeper feeling of communicating, and that's icing on the cake. Plus, you might get some other parent more interested in helping his or her son, and that's super. Finally, tell them to read this book.

HOW TO DEAL WITH THE COACH

I hope you will have read this book and practiced with your child for a few years before you even meet your child's first coach. Then you can offer your help as an assistant, or even sign up for the top job. At six to eight years old, there is not a lot of skill on the field to worry about, and it is a good starting place for inexperienced coaches.

Otherwise, I suggest you find a way to get involved. When the coach calls, offer whatever help you can give. If your job prohibits weekdays, offer to help on weekends. Many coaches will be happy for it. Some odd birds don't want help, so there's not much you can do . . . officially, but you can still work with your child at home.

Just walk up to the coach at practice and ask if you can help. Suggest taking a few kids off to the side to have a catch. You can back up the batters for foul-pops, or help with outfield practice. You can supply some water for breaks. Offer to help with phone calls. Some parents just like to sit and watch practice. I don't mind, most coaches won't either. Besides, it will help you become aware of areas where your child can use some improvement.

If the coach is a negative person, and you will probably get one for your son at some point, you should let the Little League board know about it. Bad coaches need to be weeded out. They can do a lot of damage. I remember one guy, he drank a lot, and I heard him berating his team after a loss in a whining, almost scary, melancholy tone. I broke it up, and reported the guy. He was not invited back.

If your child is playing the minimum, but only the minimum, be fair before you approach the coach. Usually, coaches are out to win, and they do play the best players. Just work a little harder, and your child may improve enough to play more. If the coach is being unfair, then talk to him about it. It is a difficult thing for all involved, so please be sure it's not just your ego complaining. And, for goodness sakes, try to keep your child out of the debate. They don't need the negative images involved. Don't get mad, the coach will take it out on your child. But don't duck it either. A few questions to the coach, nicely stated, will help.

WARMING UP

Muscles are like bubblegum, I tell my team, they need to stretch slowly or they tear. So warmups are essential. I like to have the players toss a few dozen balls softly back and forth, do some jumping jacks, jog a few hundred yards, do four to six thirty-yard wind sprints, and at least twenty pushups.

Pushups are the best baseball exercise. They give wrist, forearm, shoulder, back, and chest strength. Great for hitting. Kids should be able to do twenty to forty. You'd be surprised how quickly they can build up to that number. I always say "get an edge," and the additional strength helps to hit the ball harder. Chin ups, wind sprints, and running up stairs are also good as parts of a regular regimen.

7.

PARENT'S CHECKLIST

Now that you have read the book, it's time to get outside and have some fun with your child. I find it useful when I coach to have a checklist of things I want to remember during practice. For instance, when a boy is batting, I glance at the checklist and it reminds me to focus on different parts of his swing. It also reminds me to keep repeating several things, like "Keep your hands up," and "Open your hips with power as you make contact," and "Look at the ball."

So here is a checklist for you to use. KEEP SAYING THESE THINGS OVER AND OVER.

HITTING

1) All kids are hitters. Tell them! It will happen with work and confidence. Celebrate improvement of any kind. Be positive.

2) Repetition is essential. They should hit some balls daily or as often as possible. Go to a batting cage. Start slow and build up when ready. Hit a few yourself.

3) Keep your eyes on the ball as it moves from pitcher to the bat. See the whole ball. Watch it spin.

4) Work on the stance. Not too much at one time.

✓ Feet as wide apart as the outside of the shoulders.

✓ Stand to rear of batter's box.

✓ Rear foot should be back a bit — farther from the plate than the front foot.

✓ Weight a bit forward, towards plate, on balls of toes, a bit more on rear foot.

✓ Bend knees a bit, enough to feel loose.

✓ Bend waist forward a bit.

✓ Hands together, an inch from the end of the bat. Use a light bat.

✓ Grip bat firmly, "feel" strength in the wrists.

✓ Hands up, even with and slightly behind the rear shoulder, about six inches out.

✓ Bat points up and back a bit towards the catcher.

✓ Back elbow up, away from body, shoulders level (or front shoulder down a bit).

✓ Chin tucked into front shoulder, front shoulder tucked towards plate and down a bit.

✓ Be still. No dancing, no wiggling bat, and (sorry, Tim Teufel) no wiggling hips. Still but not stiff.

5) The Swing.

✓ Get a good pitch, in the strike zone.

✓ Step into the pitch, towards the pitcher, driving off the back toe.

✓ Swing level, almost coming down on ball, never uppercut. Keep head and front shoulder down. Move hands directly at the ball.

✓ Don't hitch, or wind up and cock the bat at beginning of swing. Hands are still, and the only movement is to the ball directly.

✓ Open the hips with power, but not too soon.

✓ Extend the arms.

✓ Hit through the ball and follow through.

✓ Consider pitching to your child on one knee, so the ball does not drop from too high.

✓ Have your child switch hit, taking a few pitches from the opposite side.

6) Bunting.

✓ Turn and face the pitcher squarely as he releases the ball.

✓ Slide top hand along the bat about one-third to one-half the distance, cradling the bat head between the thumb and next finger.

✓ Keep the head of the bat high, coming down to the ball.

✓ Let the ball hit the bat, guiding the ball down the third base line.

✓ Spring from the batter's box immediately as you make contact.

✓ Don't look at the ball, just run like the dickens.

FIELDING

1) Catching.

✓ Have a catch. It's fun. Do it regularly.

✓ Quickly get under pop-ups, catch the ball above the head, fingers up, palms out, in the web of the glove. Use both hands. Err on the side of being too deep; it's easier to run in than it is to backpedal. If you must run back, turn and run instead of running backwards. Use a rubber ball at first.

✓ Get in front of grounders, spread legs, get glove down, bend knees, body low, weight forward, scoop ball into gut, hands soft, challenge ball affirmatively. Don't come up too soon, keep head down.

✓ Get a decent glove; this is critically important. Take care of it.

2) Throwing.

✓ Repetition is key. Have a catch.

✓ Push off same foot as throwing arm.

✓ Get set and balanced.

✓ Point other foot and shoulder at target.

✓ Reach back and extend arm with throw.

✓ Grip ball with two fingers on top. Ball shouldn't be too far back in palm.

✓ Look at target's glove, throw as level as possible. Throw hard unless target is close, then throw underhand.

✓ Outfielders should never hold the ball. Throw it in to cut-off immediately.

✓ Throw ahead of the lead runner, to the cut-off.

3) Rundowns.

✓ Get the runner to commit first.

✓ Run the runner back to prior base.

✓ Hold ball high, faking throw.

✓ Receiving fielder inside of base. Tag low.

✓ Other fielders back-up.

RUNNING AND SLIDING

1) Running Bases.

✓ Find a position that fits your child's speed.

✓ Run wind sprints to strengthen legs.

✓ Run on the balls of the toes, head and shoulders forward, arms churning.

✓ Know where the ball is, always try to anticipate the chance to go to the next base.

✓ Plant left foot on inside of base and lean into the turn (either foot is okay).

✓ Try to draw the throw, fake advancing to next base, make things happen, get people's attention.

2) Sliding.

✓ Practice on a large piece of cardboard, no shoes.

✓ Right leg tucked in under the left.

✓ Slide flat on the butt, avoid turning on side.

✓ Stay low, flat, low, flat, low, flat.

✓ Don't break fall with the hand.

✓ Slide away from the ball.

BASEBALL POSITIONS

1) Catcher.

✓ For gutsy kids or slower players. Get used to the crouch, on toes, squatting, not on one knee.

✓ Don't get too far back from the plate.

✓ Let the ball come to the glove, fingers up if high, down if low, hands soft.

✓ Free hand behind the back. Fist clenched.

✓ Control the pitcher, slow him down, keep him loose and strong and focus him on your glove.

✓ Look for fielders out of position.

✓ Block pitches in the dirt.

✓ Practice "quickness" on steals — retrieve ball, snatch and fire in one motion.

✓ Tag at plate low, block plate, helmet off, two hands.

✓ Practice foul tips.

2) First Baseman.

✓ Great for lefties, tall kids.

✓ Get to bag quickly, touch bag with foot opposite glove hand.

✓ Don't stretch until you see path of throw, then stretch to meet it.

✓ Go get bad throws, leave the base if necessary.

✓ Practice throws in the dirt (wear catcher's gear if available).

✓ Go for balls in the hole.

✓ Lob to pitcher, show her the ball, lead them slightly.

✓ Practice foul pops.

✓ Once the runner has second base, move into the infield to help out.

3) Second Base.

✓ Good glove, quick, does not need arm strength.

✓ Stay low, weight forward (see FIELDING).

✓ Know where you are going to throw the ball.

✓ Cut-off on outfield balls to right side.

✓ Pivot man on double plays.

✓ Primary receiver on infield pop-up to right side.

✓ Cover first base on bunts to right side.

✓ Back up shortstop on steals.

4) Shortstop.

✓ Good glove, strong arm, leader (see FIELDING and Second Base).

✓ Play deep in the hole.

✓ Practice quick transition from catch to throw.

✓ Cut off for left side of outfield, or on any play to third base.

✓ Primary receiver on infield pop-ups, can call off any one.

✓ Hold runners on third on grounders before throwing to first base.

5) Third Base.

✓ Good learning place, not a great deal of action, need a strong arm.

✓ Need to make plays on steal, must stop the ball primarily, then tag low.

✓ See FIELDING, and other infield positions.

6) Outfield.

✓ Most action is to the right side, right fielder needs strongest arm.

✓ See FIELDING section on catching pop-ups.

✓ Don't hold the ball, throw immediately to the cut-off.

✓ Use rubber balls for practice at young ages.

✓ Block outfield grounders, lower body to one knee.

✓ Back up base in front of you on steals, especially left fielder.

7) Pitcher.

✓ Don't practice too much, arm will burn out, be sure to get rest.

✓ Start from same spot and position, consistency is key.

✓ Grip ball with fingers, ball away from palm, address batter, hands at side, take a breath.

✓ Rock the body and begin the windup.

✓ Lift front knee straight up, hands overhead, look at strike zone.

✓ Reach straight back with ball, kick front leg out towards batter, stretch, drive hard with back leg, lunge towards batter, whip open the left shoulder, extend the throwing arm, throw over the top, open up hips and come down hard with front foot, follow through gracefully. These are separate moves, but all flowing together.

✓ Consistency, gracefulness, smoothness, confidence are keys.

✓ Take your time, don't rush in between pitches, get into a rhythm.

✓ Know your batters, challenge them, throw strikes.

✓ Cover first base on grounders to the first base side.

✓ Come home on wild pitches or passed balls.

That's it. That's all I know about coaching baseball. I wish you and your child a happy, healthy, and fulfilling relationship, and I wish him or her a lot of fun at a great game. Now, let's play ball!

POEM

OH MY GOSH, I'M UP!

My gosh, he throws the ball so hard, and very wild, too!
It could go right through my head and turn it all to goo!
My knees are shaking. I may faint, I wish I wasn't born.
I think my mother closed her eyes, I feel my father's scorn.

My gut is churning in and out, maybe I have the flu
Good grief, what am I doing here, I don't know what to do.
Gosh! He just missed Mickey with a fastball high and tight!
Pretty soon he'll have my head right there within his sight.

Oh my gosh, I'm up, he just hit Mickey with the ball!
My glance back to my coach asks if he think's I am too small.
The pitcher's looking at me, Oh No! I see him grin!
He doesn't even care that he hit Mickey on the chin!

He winds up and delivers, he aimed right at my head!
"Strike one!" exclaims the ump, I stand back up, my face is red.
Oh just please let me live today, I promise to be good.
I'll mind my ma, and do my chores, and eat all of my food.

Again it comes right at me! I duck down to my knee.
"Strike two!" He must be blind this ump I'm sure he cannot see.
Here it comes again and I just swat at it in fear.
I heard a thud and somehow got my first hit of the year.

Now here I am at first base, my mother's eyes open,
Gee I feel great, the game is late, I won't get up again.

Jack McCarthy, 1988

TOMORROW!

INDEX

A

Advancing the extra base, 69
Appeal, 62
Arm burnout, in pitchers, 95

B

Backstop, 62
Balk, 62
Ball, 62
Base bag, 62
Basics, 17-32, 105-6
    of hitting, 17-32
    when to learn, 105-6
Bat grip, 23
Bat speed, 23
Bat weight, 23
Batter's box, 63
    dimensions (diagram), 58-9
Batting cage, 16
Batting glove, 16
Batting position, 19
Batting swing, 28-32
Batting tees, 34-5
Baylor, Don, 19
Behavior at games, 107-8
Breaking ball, 63
Bullpen, 63
Bunting, 36-7, 113
    (photographs), 37

C

Calling for the ball, 89
Carew, Rod, 19

Catch, 63
    rules affecting, 63
    types of, 63
Catcher, 75-80, 114-5
    blocking low pitches
        (photographs), 78
    handling foul tips, 79
    handling plays at the plate
        (photographs), 80
    stance and mechanics, 76-7
    throwing out baserunners, 79
Catching, 113
Catching fly balls, 40-3
    misjudging, 41-2
Catching pop-ups, 40-2
Catching the ball, 40
    developing confidence, 40
    grounders, 43-7
    importance of repetitive practice,
        40
Change-up, 103
Checklists for parents, 111-7
    bunting, 113
    catcher, 114-5
    catching, 113
    fielding, 113-4
    first base, 115
    outfield, 116
    pitcher, 116-7
    rundowns, 114
    running and sliding, 114
    second base, 115
    shortstop, 116

Checklists for parents, cont.
  swing, 112
  third base, 116
  throwing, 113-4
Choke-up, 63
Clark, Jack, 19
Coach, relating to, 108-9
Coaching, problems with parents, 10
Confidence, 11, 13-4
  building, 11
  the "soul" of good hitting, 13-4
Count, 64
Crane, 64
Cut-off man, hitting the, 51-4
  (photographs), 53, 54

D

Dead ball, 64
Defense, 39
  not enough coaching emphasis on, 39
Defensive swing, 15
Diamond, 64
Double play, 64, 88-9
Double play pivot, 86
Doubt and fear, effect on hitting ability, 15
Dugout, 64

E

Embarrassment, fear of, 15
Equipment, 35
Error, 64
Eye-hand coordination, 43

F

Fastball, sinking, 102
Fear, of being hit by pitch, 28
Fear and doubt, effect on hitting ability, 15
Field dimensions, 57-8
Field layout, Little League (diagrams), 58-9
Fielding, 39-56, 113-4
  fly balls, 40-3
  grounders, 43-7
    problems, 44
  pop-ups, 40-2
  rundown plays, 55-6

First base, 80-3, 115
  fielding foul pop-ups, 82
  fielding grounders, 81-3
  fielding poor throws, 82-3
  lob to pitcher (photographs), 83
  plays with pitcher, 83
  stretch, 81
Fly balls, catching, 40-3
Follow through, 64
Force play, 64
Forfeit, 64
Foul, 65
Fungo, 65
Fungo practice, 42-3
  easier to throw rather than hit ball, 42

G

Gamer, 65
Glossary of terms, 61-6
Glove, 47
  batting, 16
  breaking it in, 47
  good quality necessary, 47
Grip, bat, 23
Grip, pitching (photograph), 100
Gripping the ball, 50
Ground rule double, 65
Grounder, 65
Grounders, fielding, 43-7
  fielding, 43-7
    drill (photograph), 46
    drills for improving reflexes, 46-7
  problems with, 44
  (photographs), 45-6

H

Hand-eye coordination, 43
Head-first sliding, 73
Hit, 65
Hit by pitch, fear of, 28
Hitting, 13-37, 111-3
  bat grip (photograph), 23
  bunting, 37-8
  child's confidence is critical, 13-4
  choking up on the bat, 23
    (photograph), 23
  coaching can help, 13
  eye and head movement, 18

Hitting, cont.
  fear of embarrassment, 15
  improper swing (photograph), 31
  improvement is possible!, 13
  keeping your eye on the ball, 17-8
  most important part of baseball,
    13
  parent's role in practice, 15-6
  problems with, 15
  proper swing (photograph), 31
  repetitive practice essential, 15-6
  seeing the ball, 18
  self-doubt, 15
  stance, 19-23
  stepping into the pitch, 29-30
  swing, 28-32
    "hitch", 32
    opening the hips, 32-3
    opening the hips
      (photographs), 33
    practicing without the ball, 30
    the stride, 29
  switch, 36
  the basics, 17-33
Hitting the cut-off man, 51-3
  (photographs), 53,54

I

Infield fly rule, 60-1
Inning, 65
Interest in baseball, developing in
  your child, 107
Interference, 65

K

Keeping your eye on the ball, 17
Knuckleball, 103

L

Lead, 66
Lead runner, throwing in front of,
  51-3
Learning the game, best age to,
  105-6
Left field, a good learning position,
  91
Little League, 10, 14, 15, 35, 70, 76,
  80, 82, 85, 91, 95, 106, 109
  getting on the team, 58-99

Little League, cont.
  official rules, 57, 60
    violations of, 60
  tie games, 61

M

"Major League" — the advanced
  Little League, 87
Mantle, Mickey, 16
Mattingly, Don, 19
Misjudging fly balls, 41-2

O

Oh My Gosh, I'm Up!, 119
Ott, Mel, 19
Outfield, 91-4, 116
  backing up second on stealing
    attempts, 93
  backing up third base
    (photograph), 94
  fielding grounders, 92-3
    (photographs), 93
  practice drills, 92

P

Parent, 10, 15-6, 17, 33-5, 43, 46,
  56, 107-9, 111-7
  behavior at games, 107-8
  checklists of things to say and do,
    111-7
    bunting, 113
    catcher, 114-5
    catching, 113
    fielding, 113-4
    first base, 115
    111-3
    outfield, 116
    pitcher, 116-7
    rundowns, 114
    running and sliding, 114
    second base, 115
    shortstop, 116
    swing, 112
    third base, 116
    throwing, 113-4
  focusing on slight improvements,
    43
  keeping your patience, 46
  knowledge of hitting basics
    important, 17

Parent, cont.
pitching hitting practice at the
child's level, 33-4
power of positive attitude, 33
problems with coaches, 10
questioning your child's playing
time, 109
relating to the coach, 108-9
role in hitting practice, 15-6
teaching and talking about
defense, 56
the exercise is good for you!, 33
tips to, 33-5
watching hitter's eye and head
movement, 18
"Pepper", 35
Pitch, 66
Pitcher, 94-103, 116-7
arm burnout, 95
usually gifted athlete, 95
Pitches, types of, 102-3
age at which to learn/throw
breaking pitches, 103
Pitching grip (photograph), 100
Pitching strategy, 101
Pitching style, 96-8
addressing the batter, 96
six parts of the pitch
(photographs), 96-7
the crane, 98
the delivery, 98
wind-up, 98
Pitching tips, 98-9
Pop-ups, 40-2
catching, 40-2
(photographs), 41
chasing down (photographs), 42
Positions, 75-103
catcher, 75-80
blocking low pitches
(photographs), 78
handling foul tips, 79
handling plays at plate
(photographs), 80
(photograph), 77
stance and mechanics, 76-7
throwing out baserunners, 79
working with the pitcher, 77-8
first base, 80-3
fielding grounders, 81-3

first base, cont.
fielding foul pop-ups, 82
fielding poor throws, 82-3
lob to pitcher (photographs), 82
plays with pitcher, 83
stretch (photographs), 81
left field, a good learning
position, 91
outfield, 91, 92-3, 94
backing up second on steal
attempts, 93
backing up third base
(photograph), 94
fielding grounders
(photographs), 93
fielding grounders, 92-3
practice drills, 92
pitcher, 94-103
arm burnout, 95
usually gifted athlete, 95
second base, 83-7
as cut-off man, 85-7
double play pivot (photograph),
86
fielding pop-ups, 85
gets the most grounders, 84
role in steal attempts, 87
tagging the runner
(photograph), 86
thinking player needed, 84
shortstop, 87-90
as cut-off man, 89
faking a throw, 89
good arm required, 87
making the double play, 88-9
often one of best athletes on
team, 88
third base, 90-1
characteristics needed, 90
making the tag, 90-1
strong arm needed, 90
Practice, necessary to improve
hitting, 15-6
Pre-Little League clinics, 35
Pushups, 109

R

Repetition, 33-4, 46
to improve fielding, 46
to improve hitting, 33-4

Rose, Pete, 19
Rules of the game, 57-66
Rundowns, 55-6, 114
Running and sliding, 67-73, 114
Running bases, 68-9
  advancing the extra base, 69
Running speed, 67

S

Saberhagen, Bret, 99
Second base, 83-7, 115
  as cut-off man, 85-7
  double play pivot (photograph),
    86
  fielding pop-ups, 85
  gets the most grounders, 84
  role in steal attempts, 87
  tagging the runner (photograph),
    86
  thinking player needed, 84
Seeing the ball, as a hitter, 18
Self-doubt, as it affects hitting, 15
Shortstop, 87-90, 116
  as cut-off man, 89
  faking a throw, 89
  good arm required, 87
  making the double play, 88-9
  often one of best athletes on
    team, 88
Sinking fastball, 102
Slider, 103
Sliding, 70-3
  head first, 73
  (photographs), 72
Speed, running, 67
Split-finger fastball, 103
Stance, hitting, 19-23, 25-7
  correct, 20-2
    left-handed hitters, 20
    right-handed hitters, 20
  front view (photographs), 21
  incorrect, 19, 25-7
    (photographs), 25-7
  instructions, 20-4

Stance, cont.
  personal styles, 19
  side view (photographs), 22
Stealing bases, 70
"Stepping into the bucket", 28
Stepping into the pitch, 29-30
Strike zone, 66
Swing, 28-33, 112
  batting, 28-32
    bad habits, 30
    "hitch", 32
    opening the hips, 32-3
    (photographs), 31
    practicing without the ball, 30
    the stride, 29
  defensive, 15
Switch hitting, 35-6

T

Tag, 66
Team, a family affair, 108
Team spirit, 11
Tees, batting, 34-5
Third base, 90-1, 116
  characteristics needed, 90
  making the tag, 90-1
  strong arm needed, 90
Throwing the ball, 47-51
  ahead of the lead runner, 51-3
  aim, 49-50
  basics, 48-51
  form (photographs), 48
  grip, 49
    (photographs), 50
  the cut-off man (photographs),
    53, 54
  the cut-off man, 51-3
  velocity, 50-1
Tie games, Little League, 61

W

Warming up, 109
Warmups, 66
Wind sprints, 67
Winning, right attitude toward, 106